Discovered T[...]
An Antholo[...]

By

Patrick Scattergood

Acknowledgements

Where would I be without my wonderful children, Cyrus and Fae? Two amazing children who help me see the wonderful magic still in the world, even though I'm a silly old person.

I have to say a huge thank you to my partner, Golda, who has put up with me locking myself away to write these stories and then being a grumpy old bear when they've gone right. They truly have the patience of all the saints combined.

And to you, my lovely readers, thank you for reading my silly little stories and for making this nerdy, awkward non-binary author feel like their words are entertaining.

I truly, truly love you all.

Also By Patrick Scattergood

Short Story Collections
Flesh Tones

Novels

The Mother Dearest Series
Mother, Dearest - Book One
The Man Who Died Twice - Book Two
Hell, as Seen from Heaven - Book Three

The Sherlock Holmes Adventures Series
The Case of the Morbid Detection

The Ballad of Cassandra

Written With Golda Evans
Time to Burn

Author Note

When I wrote my short story collection, *Flesh Tones*, I really had it in mind that it would be *one and done*, as they call it.

Once it was done and released into the world, I was blown away by how much people liked my short stories. It hadn't been something I'd done before, but I loved stepping out of my comfort zone.

The stories in that collection all followed the theme of death. Cheerful, I know, but I wanted to tell stories with that theme while managing to keep them as varied as possible. I truly feel that death is seen as a big taboo. That's why I told stories from the points of view of an elderly lady in a nursing home, a man adrift in space, a serial killer's victims, and more.

This collection's theme is a loose one, but it's one of discoveries, both good and bad. I hope that you enjoy this collection as much as I enjoyed writing the stories. I am really proud of each one.

Trans rights are human rights.

Patrick Scattergood
October 2023

Enjoy the Silence

Eivor had always thought the city, in which she found herself living, was trying far too hard to be like New York; it had even stolen its nickname of being the "city that never sleeps," and that had never sat well with her.

From the very moment that they had found themselves here, drawn into the heart of the city by a compulsion to strike out and make a name for themselves as artists, she had been assaulted by the noise that surrounded her and ran through every inch of the place. The blaring horns of impatient taxi drivers, the cacophony of street vendors hawking their wares, the shouts of people offering companionship but at a price. All those and more mixed together to create an unbreakable symphonic wall of sound, one that threatened to tumble down and crush her under its debris.

After a few days here, Eivor had come to begrudgingly accept the noise. If anything, it had become somewhat of a soundtrack to her existence, not that she'd had even the smallest shred of choice in the matter. The chaos that the never-ending voices and echoes brought with them also brought a strange sense of calm. It was like an invisible thread holding her thoughts together and stopping them from turning dark and hurtful.

As if summoned by the quiet in her mind, the myriad scars that criss-crossed her arms began to throb, and each time they did, a bolt of pain danced across her skin. Rubbing the palm of a hand over them didn't help, nor did shutting her eyes and counting to ten, so Eivor resorted to the one thing that had always worked. She tried to ignore them until they stopped.

She grimaced as she pushed herself off of the bed in the tiny apartment she called home. It wasn't much, but it was her and decorated as well as what her meagre income would allow. In one corner stood the guitar she used when she went out busking, and in another was a battered chest of drawers that she had found dumped in the street. It had taken a few attempts and a lot of stops on the way for her to carry it home and place it there after a good clean. It held the few sets of clothes that she owned, and in the bottom drawer were the scraps of paper with her songs scribbled on them in her messy handwriting. On top of the drawers sat a dented and scratched record player. Only one of the two speakers worked, and even that one made an incessant hissing sound while it did, but it meant she could listen to the one thing she owned that meant something, the record collection. She kept them in a large, but dirty, old crate that she'd somehow managed to steal from a nearby pub without anyone noticing.

As she reached over and flicked through the collection of vinyl, Eivor smiled. She wasn't even sure why she was looking through them, one at a time, because she knew already which one she was going to play tonight. Perhaps it was just her way of showing gratitude to the music that she knew had saved her life on more than one occasion; perhaps it was just another one of her little superstitious quirks that she'd inherited from her mother, but as she pulled out the album she wanted, a contented sensation rushed through her.

Walking over to the record player, she flipped the album over in her hands to read the track-listing. Violator by Depeche Mode had long since been one of her favourite albums, especially after she had taken her step-dad's copy of it with her when she walked out, and as she pulled out the record and placed it on the turntable, his mocking insults tried to push themselves into her thoughts. Shaking her head in an effort to silence them, she moved the arm of the record player over and onto the record and sighed in relief as the first seconds of World in My Eyes started to play.

Falling backwards and letting her entire body bounce onto the bed at an ungainly angle, Eivor let the lyrics and music wash over her. When she would lose herself in music, it didn't matter if it was her own songs or someone else's; it was the one time that she felt safe in her own skin. It was the one time that the pain of the past that she had run away from couldn't reach her. She felt alive, content, and happy—something that just didn't happen to someone like her unless it was some shitty low-budget movie.

When Eivor had moved here, she hadn't known a single person until, one night spent wandering in the dark thanks to the nightmares that wouldn't leave her alone, she found a small record store, one that always seemed to be open no matter the time of day or night, and it had fast become her safe space, a place where the voices in her head were silent and she could just be.

It was the owner who struck up the conversation first. He had been impressed with the faded Blondie t-shirt she was wearing and started to talk about the band and their songs, even ones she hadn't even known existed. Before she knew it, hours had passed and she had made a friend, her first in a new city. Now, as she lay on the bed listening to the voice of Dave Gahan telling her to reach out and touch faith, Eivor felt a sudden urge to put her boots on and wander down to the shop.

Sitting up, Eivor found herself staring at the record player as the vinyl went round and round as the songs continued. It was a huge cliché that music could help a person, but, to her, it had always been true. It was something that gave her the strength to be herself when she was standing in the streets, guitar in hand, and singing her songs. Not that every night was like that. Sometimes she would go home without a single coin or note on her guitar. Sometimes she would go home with a shouted insult still ringing in her ears. Other times, and these were the lucky ones, she would go home with enough money to have some food in the apartment, pay one of the bills, or even buy a new record.

"The life of a rock star," she said quietly to himself as she waited for the last song on the album to fade away before putting the arm of the record player back on its stand and the album back in its sleeve. Placing it back in the crate, Eivor smiled before making her way towards the door. "Don't misbehave while I'm gone," she said, smirking, at the crate before walking out and closing the door behind her.

It felt weird, almost wrong, walking down the corridor without the trusty weight of her guitar on her back. It was her comfort blanket. Her loud, sticker-covered comfort blanket, but still she made her way through the complex and out onto the street.

Eivor took a moment to watch as people rushed about their daily business. There wasn't a single spot where there wasn't movement or noise of some kind, and it came close to leaving her overwhelmed. Rushing away from the apartment building, she pulled her hood up as far as it would go, kept her head down, and tried to get to the shop as quickly as she could. The knowledge that, once inside, there would be row upon row of vinyl to look through kept her grounded as she made her way through the thick crowds of loud people.

It was almost by instinct alone that she looked up and realised that she had arrived. The outside of the shop itself didn't look anything special. If you hadn't been inside before, then you wouldn't even know it was a record shop. That was the beauty of the place. It was like a secret built into brick and mortar. A place that was both there and imagined.

She took a cursory glance over her shoulder and then stepped inside, hoping that the ringing of the bell above the door didn't alert anyone else to the place or ruin her time here. She wasn't one for small talk; she wasn't one for talking much at all, but here was her special place.

A low, wet-sounding echo of a throat being cleared made her look up, and the vision of the old man in front of her made her smile. Mike, the owner of the shop, with his near-silver-coloured beard that made him look like a wizard, stood proudly behind the till area and waved his hands around at the displays.

"Welcome, weary traveller, to the home of music. The cave of vinyl wonders, the palace of poets, and the lair of lyricists."

Eivor laughed. He always did this, no matter how many times she visited the shop, and she loved it every time.

"You will discover bands that you've never heard of before, songs that will dance in your ears and become tears that roll down your cheeks. You will fall in love with singers long dead and with bands long since disbanded. This is the home of the music, and with it, I welcome you."

She found that she'd been mouthing along with his greeting the entire time and looked at the floor shyly as he walked towards her, his arms outstretched in affection.

"Eivor, my darling fellow music lover. How the fucking devil are ya?"

The way his thick Irish accent came through whenever he greeted her was something that she had always loved hearing. It had a way about it that made her feel safe, welcome, and included. Looking around the shop briefly, wondering when the last time it had been decorated was, she then turned to face him, a sly smile forming on her face.

"I'm good. Thanks, pal. Same as always, skint, tired, hungry, but full of songs about being all of those."

"Ah, yes, the best way to be, girl, the best way to be. It's where the music finds its heart. Sometimes when the singer is still alive, if they're lucky, and sometimes when they've jumped off a bridge. Either of which is fine, although the latter makes the albums sell faster."

There it was, Mike's dark sense of humour coming through once again. It was just another thing that she found charming about the man. He was old enough to be her father, but he was the complete opposite of the man who raised her in every possible way. For starters, he wasn't a massive, self-centred arse-hole. That was always a good way to be, although these days that seemed to be sorely lacking in the people she met.

"Well, I don't have an album, nor do I have any intention of jumping off a bridge in an effort to promote it if I did."

Mike laughed heartily and pointed his fingers at her, making pew-pew noises before gesturing at the walls.

"Got some new ones up there, love. Although new is an optional term. Some fella was throwing em away. Said vinyl is dead, and so are the bands. Took em all off his hands for less than a fancy dinner down town."

Mike seemed rather pleased with himself for having engaged in such a cheap business transaction, and then, snatching up a thick book about Jimi Hendrix, he began to read. After a brief moment, he slapped his palm against his head and looked towards Eivor.

"Oh, before I forget, lass, are you still okay to watch the shop for me next Tuesday?"

"Of course."

"Fantastic. You're a good one," he replied before swiftly going back to his book, muttering about Hendrix being the god of guitars to himself.

Intrigued by the records that Mike had pointed her towards, Eivor started to thumb through them slowly, taking her time to try to find a hidden gem amongst them. It was an eclectic set of records, something Mike was well known for, with the mixture including gospel, 80s hair metal, and even a folk album by a guy with a beard that rivalled even his.

The records that adorned the walls all seemed to be looking down at her as she looked at the new arrivals, watching as she stopped at an album that had caught her eye.

On the cover stood a solitary man, his facial features blurred and unrecognisable. The way he stood, with his hands by his sides, made him look like he had the weight of the world on his shoulders, and she pulled it out to get a closer look. Emblazoned across the image were jagged words that looked almost handwritten. Enjoy the silence. Surely that was the name of the album, and as she traced the shapes of the letters with the tip of her finger, Eivor became very aware of someone whispering those very same three words in her ear. When she turned around, she saw that, other than Mike being lost in his Jimi Hendrix book, she was completely alone in the shop and clutched the album close to her chest.

"You found something good there, Eivor? A treasure amongst the dusty songs that nobody knows exists or even remembers?"

He was giving her the hard sell, but it wasn't needed. Eivor already knew that she had to have this album; she just had to have it. It was like an addict wanting their next fix, and she would give him anything to own it.

Seeing the excited glint in her eyes, Mike grinned like a proud father and pointed at the record in her arms.

"Tell you what. You take it home, lass, give it a listen, and if you like it, then come back here and gissa note or two. How does that sound?"

Eivor barely gave him enough time to register that she had said thank you before she was out of the shop and running back to her apartment. Each step, each move forward, brought with it that voice repeating the name of the album.

Closing her apartment door behind her, she could barely remember how she had gotten back home so quickly. She rushed over to the record player, placed the album on the turntable, and lifted the arm, but hesitated for a moment. There was something about the cover that seemed to be beckoning her to look at it again. The image of the faceless man standing in a vast, empty space. It screamed loneliness, sadness, and even the loss of hope, but she knew she had to listen to the songs.

Turning the album over in her hands, she was surprised to find that there was no track-listing at all, just those three words repeated over and over again in a messy, scratched style. Eivor shrugged, dropped the cover onto her bed, placed the arm on the record, and waited for it to rotate.

Laying back on the bed, she swore as the light above her flickered, but it was soon forgotten when the music began to play.

For the first time since she had rescued it from a dirty, stained skip, the record player's one working speaker wasn't hissing through the music. The more surprising thing was the simple fact that the other speaker was now working, and the melodic, otherworldly music drifted around her room. She closed her eyes, letting the music wash over her, letting it cling to her body like a well-worn but comfy sweater. Around her, it was as if the whole world had begun to drift away into nothingness, leaving her alone with only the music for company. The haunting lyrics and the ethereal melody all left her feeling strangely comforted and content.

A realisation crossed her thoughts, one that stepped into her consciousness, gently reminding her of an introvert being stuck at a party and trying to make conversation. This was the only time that she had experienced silence—a profound, beautiful silence. It was a silence that embraced her like a long-lost old friend, one that promised Eivor tranquillity and solitude of the purest kind, luring her to sleep deeply.

When she awoke, the sun was streaming through her window, illuminating the entire room with a warm and gentle glow. A happiness swirled in her head like a child dancing, and Eivor sat up, yawned, and swung her legs out of bed.

She threw some clothes on, and in her excitement, she ran outside with her guitar on her back. Setting up in her normal spot, she opened her guitar case in front of her and played, the pick gliding over the guitar strings gracefully and delicately.

It wasn't until midway through the second song that she realised something was wrong— something was different. The entire city, with its hustle and bustle demands placed on the heads of its inhabitants and its incessant need to control everything by its sheer volume of sound, was silent. Completely, and utterly silent. The street hawkers, the other buskers, the hyperactive children—there wasn't a single noise to be found.

Running to the record shop, she found the door locked tight. Screaming as loudly as she could, she hammered on the door, feeling it shake under the impact of her fists, but still nothing. Even as her knuckles started to bleed from the force of her hitting the wood, the warm, viscous liquid ran down her hands. Eivor knew she was silenced. Her scream, her attacking the door—none of it made a single damned bit of difference. She heard none of it.

"Mike. Let me in. Please. Something is wrong. Let me in; I'm begging you."

As her mouth moved and Eivor was sure that she was saying the pleas as loudly as she could muster, the loneliness in the silence came at her, forcing her to her knees as the tears ran down her face.

"Mike. Please hear me. That's all I'm asking. Hear one word, just one."

Looking up, Eivor could see translucent shadows moving around her as her memories started to jumble together, destroying the brief sense of serenity she had brought. As quickly as they had appeared, they were gone, and she slumped against the record shop door. The coldness of the wood comforted her for a moment as she looked around, wondering what to do next.

Each second she sat here, each moment she was alone, was the longest of her life. Again, she tried to call out for Mike or for anyone, but her voice was gone. Despite being outside and despite being alone, the atmosphere felt suffocating and violent in its attempts to drive her insane. She had no way out, no way to fix whatever this was. Eivor wasn't even sure that any of this was real.

A shadowy figure moved in the periphery of her vision, but when she turned her head, it was gone. The whispered voice, the only thing she could still hear, still continued to say those three words.

Desperation began to take hold of her, making her entire body feel stiff with panic, until the door opened behind her and she tumbled into the record store, ending up in an untidy pile covered by the vinyl collections that had adorned the walls of Mike's shop.

"What the fuck are you doing, lass?"

Eivor didn't need to be able to hear to know what Mike had said. The look on his face more than made up for that as she tried to throw the records off of her so she could get to her feet. He looked just as panicked as she felt but offered his hand towards her, pulling her up.

Enjoy the silence.

Those three words. If Eivor knew anything, it was that she was sick and tired of hearing them. If she could click her fingers and find herself back in bed listening to Depeche Mode, she would have done so instantly. Hell, she knew full well that she would give up anything to hear just one lyric, even just one word.

Words are very unnecessary; they can only do harm.

It was ironic beyond belief that it was those words that came to her mind right now, but at least it was better than being mocked with the three whispered words from the album she had taken home.

Feeling Mike tapping her arm, Eivor looked at him with tears in her eyes. All she could manage was to shake her head and point at where she had gotten the record from. Just the small movement of her hand felt like she was trying to move a large weight. That was when she saw it; the change in Mike's facial expression worried her. He seemed different and changed somehow, but she couldn't put her finger on why or how.

Mike turned away from her and walked over to the display, waving his hand in her direction to tell her to follow.

"I tried to help. Truly, I did. I saw you suffering. I saw you overwhelmed by the very world you were trying to entertain. This wasn't meant to happen. You were supposed to be happy."

She couldn't hear what he was saying, but the sadness and guilt that were coming from him couldn't have been clearer if they had been coming from one of the neon signs outside.

He turned to face her once, and she lunged, grabbing him by his Pink Floyd t-shirt and pulling him close enough for her to be able to smell something strange coming from him.

"To regain that which you lost, you first must give up what you need."

Eivor screwed her face up in confusion as she heard his voice for the first time since coming into the store. It sounded exactly like the whispers telling her to enjoy the silence, and a festering anger gripped her stomach, making her nauseous.

"But what do you need?"

The guitar on her back felt heavier than ever before, weighing her down as she looked at Mike, and the world around them melted away.

The sounds came rushing back, and she fell to her knees, blood flowing from her ears. Eivor screamed out in pain, and her voice mixed with the hundreds of sounds that she had been missing.

"See? I told you I was trying to help. This is what happens when I don't. You can't cope. I hate seeing you suffer like this, but you know what they say. The road to Hell is paved with good intentions, right?"

Mike clicked his fingers, and the sounds stopped instantly, save for Eivor's gentle and delicate sobbing as she lay on the floor of the record shop.

"I'll let you hear me for now, but let's see how we go. I don't want you to be in any more pain than you absolutely have to be."

Enjoy the silence.

There they were again. Those three words that had brought her back here were hissed at her, as if full of venom. Each word and each syllable sent a shiver down her spine and made the hairs on her arms stand up.

Enjoy the silence.

Slowly, and with each minuscule movement feeling like a battle in itself, Eivor managed to look up at Mike. There was a sharp, stabbing pain in her chest that radiated out to every part of her body, but she met his joke with a stern, determined one of her own.

"Why are you doing this? All I wanted was to hear music above the noise of the world, to hear the lyrics and the emotions. Why have you taken that from me?"

"You speak to me as if it were a punishment. You speak as if the silence and quietness that I have given you are anything but the gift they were intended to be. I'm trying to save you and your mind from the constant bombardment that the world subjects you to. The advertisements, the insults, and the never-ending flow of lies and fabrications from the media. It's all just noise. It's all just a mess that drowns those unlucky enough to be caught in its rip tide."

Eivor couldn't take her eyes away from Mike. He had always been kind to her and had always welcomed her to his shop, making it feel like a home away from home, but this wasn't him; this wasn't right. It was a punishment, an abuse, not the gift that he was making it out to be.

Mike stepped forward and held out his arms as if to embrace her, but she moved away from him, her determination to not let him twist her mind into what he wanted to be unwavering.

"You sound like a fucking politician trying to get re-elected."

"Then at least I know what my public wants. A respite from the bullshit that chokes and assaults them on a daily basis."

The eerie stillness around them had left the record shop feeling like a prison, and Mike was most certainly the guard.

Again, he stepped towards her, and as he did, his entire body began to stretch and bend into a grotesque photocopy of what a person was meant to look like. His arms and legs stretched out, and his face ripped as it stretched over his now longer facial features. Reaching out an elongated finger towards her, Mike grinned, and saliva dripped from his pointed teeth.

"You, your kind, all of this—it's just another layer to the shit pile that grows ever larger, aren't you? I have tried and tried to make the lives I touch better, quieter, and kinder. What do I get in return? Berated by a person who plays third-rate songs, ripped off from musicians much better than her, one that comes here begging me for some kind of connection that doesn't leave her drained. It's pathetic. I should have seen it coming from a mile away, but no, I thought you were different. Truly, I did. Now," he paused for a moment as he raised his outstretched hand up to the sky, "enjoy the silence."

The click of his now long, misshaped fingers sounded like an explosion in front of her, and Eivor covered her eyes instinctively to protect herself. Instantly, the whole world around her was silent once more, and when she opened her eyes, she was surrounded by a bright, pure white expanse of nothingness.

Beginning to panic, she tried to call out, tried to scream out Mike's name, to scream out any name she could think of, but nothing came out of her mouth. She screamed until her throat was raw and she could taste the metallic tang of the blood in her mouth.

Knowing that it was useless to call for help and that it was all useless and futile at best, she curled into a ball when she lay down and sobbed. Her whole body shook with the force of the tears that forced themselves from her eyes, each one feeling like acid as it touched her skin.

A rush of memories swirled through her mind like the waves of a storm-swept ocean. A symphony of voices, of the lost sounds of the city, all mixed into a symphony, a glorious cacophony of sounds before dying away for the last time.

As Eivor took her last breath, her hand fell away from her chest, hitting the ground. On her wrist, in stark ink-coloured letters, were three words—the title of her favourite song.

Enjoy the silence.

One Fall to a Finish

My name is Jason Hanson, and I was a professional wrestler for over 50 years. I'm 71 now and feel every bump, every scar, and every chair shot that I took during that career.

Now, armed with only my memories, I spend most of my days sitting on the porch in the wooden swing that I made myself, just watching the day go by. It's that inner peace, that sense of contentment, that it gives me. When the breeze is just right, my mind wanders back to that time in the ring, and a smile crosses my face.

When I was a young child living in a small town in Tennessee, wrestling was huge. Stories of feats of superhuman strength would come through the radio, thrilling us all and creating images in our heads of real-life superheroes fighting against the most brutal of enemies in an effort to win that big gold belt to cement their legacy.

Most had the movies playing at the little movie house in town, but not me; those stories on the radio were all I needed. If I was lucky, a neighbour, one of the few in town who owned a tiny, black-and-white television set, would call me over to watch wrestling on one of the local channels. There were times when I thought I would explode from excitement at watching the men throw each other around.

Even though my family was well known in town because my father had been a local wrestler before an injury halted his career, we didn't have a lot of money. We also didn't have a lot of say in the matter if we were to follow in his footsteps.

My mother, on the other hand, was protective of me. I was as thin as a rake, had never been in a fight before, and was prone to clumsy accidents, and she worried that I would hurt myself or worse, so, much to my dad's annoyance, she made it a rule that I wasn't to begin the full training until I was fifteen.

As soon as that day came, under the watchful eyes of my father, I began my journey.

As I, the youngest of three boys, had shown the most interest, he soon put me in training. My brothers went along with it; they went through the motions, but their hearts were never in it; mine, however, pounded with the excitement of one day getting into that right and making my father proud.

It was hard and painful, and the training left me with cuts and bruises all over my body, but I felt more alive than I had before. The aches, the pains— I wore those suckers like badges of honour. In my mind, they told the story of my quest to be the mightiest warrior that the ring had ever seen.

I stuck with it out of stubbornness and a sense of duty to my father, but my brothers soon dropped out. It just wasn't their thing, and I was okay with that. It was my thing, my quest, and my dream.

Soon, thanks to his connections with the local wrestling group, I was in the ring. I don't look at those matches with rose-coloured glasses. I was terrible, I was awkward, and most of the time, the crowd laughed at my attempts to do the simplest of moves, but I was living my dream.

For the next year or so, I was used as an enhancement wrestler. The better and more popular, or hated, wrestlers beat me up and pinned me down while I was there. That was my job, and I was okay with that. I was in the ring, and that was all that mattered to me. Eventually, I began to improve; I began to get more fluid and confident, and the crowd started to notice too. There weren't so many jeers or boos when I walked to the ring. Some of the audience even cheered when they saw me.

Then came the day for me to win my first match. My mother was in the crowd, reacting with worry to each punch, kick, and move I took. That was my skill, you see, to make the audience think I was getting broken in half each time I was grabbed, and it worked. Then, in the middle of my opponent setting me up for a piledriver, their finishing move that would drive my head into the mat, I rolled him up into a pin and heard the referee's hand slap the mat three times to signal that I had won.

Nothing after that moment mattered to me; I felt like the all-conquering hero. I felt like a champion. To the others in the crowded locker room, it was just a fluke win to drive forward a storyline, but to me, it was the best thing that had ever happened to me.

I spent the rest of my time there, winning the odd match or two here and there, but I'd reached my ceiling. Then the unexpected happened. I got my big break, one that some of the others felt was undeserved, but I knew in my heart that I'd worked as hard as my body would allow me to.

The talent scout had seen me take one of my well-rehearsed beatings and then come back to win the match, shocking my opponent and getting a loud, raucous reaction from the crowd in the run-down space we used for our shows. He wanted me to travel to Memphis, the home of wrestling in my eyes, to try out for a promotion that ran televised shows weekly.

I went there, hitchhiking the entire way, and had my tryout match against one of their wrestlers, who happily sat on the lower end of their roster, and they were impressed.

My opponent, a big, stoic masked man named Tormentor Dan, even put in a good word for me, saying that I would be good cannon fodder for him and his tag partner, an even bigger masked man called Brutal Bert. It must have worked, because they offered me a contract on the spot.

It was one of their lowest-paid contracts, but it still made me feel like I'd made it. I was being paid to wrestle on television. I felt like a superstar, and, in my own mind at least, I was.

Each and every match I had, win or lose, I put my all into it. I was given a new ring name, Captain Tom Riley, and the gimmick of being a dirty-looking sea captain who had come to the promotion in the hopes of winning titles and taking them for his own treasure. I was on top of the world.

No matter how many matches I had in Memphis as I slowly made my way up the ranks, I never forgot the first time I had a televised match.

The crowd was roaring, enjoying every match they had seen that night; the lights were blinding, and I'd been told that I was going to win. It would be the start of a long storyline with Tormentor Dan and Brutal Bert, who, together, were called the Bully Squad.

I was going to come out to be the tag partner of a cape and mask-wearing good guy called The Memphis Monsoon, whose tag partner had been attacked earlier in the show, rendering him unable to compete. Then we would go from show to show, battling one another in tag matches, singles matches, and pretty much any other type of match the promoter could think of.

The storyline went well, and for a short time, Monsoon and I were the tag champions too, but then we lost them to a young, up-and-coming team called The Bad Seed, and we went our separate ways.

I rose higher in the rankings, growing more popular with the audience than I'd ever hoped I could be, and eventually I was given a chance to fight for their main championship.

It was a back-and-forth match, with me giving my all against their number one heel, a villain named Divinity. His character was that of an arrogant man who thought he was God's gift to women and that all men wanted to be him, and he played it well. Even though we were friends away from the ring, even I wanted to punch him in the face when he played the character.

The funny thing was that the faces and the heels, the good guys and the bad guys, weren't meant to be seen in public together. It was a way for the audience to suspend their disbelief for a little bit longer, and we mostly adhered to the rule, but when we found out that Divinity's wife was going to be having a baby, we knew that we had to celebrate that.

We went to a bar out of town in the hopes we wouldn't be seen together, and for the first hour or so, that worked. We were having a great time, drinking and eating some of the best burgers I'd ever eaten in my life, when we heard the one thing we had hoped to avoid.

Now, keep in mind that out of our group, only three of us were the good guys, and the other five were known as the villains on the shows we put on.

"Captain! Divinity's behind you!"

I hung my head and nodded at the two men next to me. We knew what we were going to have to do. We were going to have to put on an impromptu show for the people watching.

Instantly, Divinity, whose real name was Simon, threw a bottle at me, deliberately missing but making enough noise to make others look up, and the bar fight was on.

We pulled our punches as best we could, but it still went over the top as our adrenaline made us think we were invincible.

A few broken chairs here, a broken table there, even a broken jukebox—thanks to an errant elbow by Tormentor Dan—and the police were soon on the scene, and we were all arrested.

Hank Baclin, the promoter, was pissed and let us know it when he came to bail us out. Money came out of our next few pay checks to pay him back, but the next few shows were sold out, with the audience wanting us to fight each other more and more after hearing reports of the bar fight.

But I digress.

The actual championship match itself was a thing of beauty. I was on top of my game, Divinity was on top of his game, and we played with the crowd's emotions like they were cheap violins and we were the conductors.

Near falls, inference by The Bully Squad, and the Memphis Monsoon running out to even the odds—everything seemed to work perfectly.

Finally, after nearly 45 minutes of us beating seven shades of hell out of one another, it was time for the ending we had planned.

I was down on the mat, breathing heavily, and feeling the brutal effects of the match. Divinity was on top of the match and had used every ounce of cheating he could get away with. He had hit me with every heavy move that he had in his arsenal and grown more and more frustrated each time I kicked out of his pin attempts.

In a sense of panic, not knowing how to put me away for the final three count, he climbed to the top rope, something he rarely did, and prepared to finish me with a match-ending elbow drop.

The audience gasped, a low ripple of shocked excitement running through them.

I watched as Divinity readied himself and then jumped. I counted in my head and rolled out of the way at the last possible moment, feeling the impact of his body on the mat where I had been only seconds earlier.

Getting to my feet and still feeling the effects of the beating he had given me, I grabbed his head and suplexed him, hooking his leg on the way over. As I clasped my fingers together, making sure he couldn't kick out, I heard the three first and then the roar of the audience a split second later.

Knowing it was out of sight of the crowd, I patted his shoulder to thank him for an amazing match before getting to my feet as the referee handed me the title belt. I lifted it high into the air and let the tears come. Some would have said it was over the top, but the emotions were real. I'd worked for this, sacrificed everything to get a run at the title, and here I was. It was finally my turn.

That set off a run of things that made me one of the busiest wrestlers Memphis had seen. I defended that belt in whatever promotion they wanted me to perform for, treating each match as if it were in front of thousands, even if it was only in front of a hundred or less. I made sure those people got the most bang for their buck and went home happy.

Word spread. More and more promotions wanted me. The money flowed like wine; I partied, I travelled, and I did everything I had always wanted to do, but that fame came at a price.

By then, I'd fallen in love with a waitress I'd met on my travels, and she had taken my breath away. We married soon after, knowing that it was everything I wanted, but I was barely home, even in the early days. I missed the births of my children. I missed too many birthdays to count. Despite being loved, it soon became one of the most lonely things I had ever felt.

As I got older, my body started to fail me; it started to break down, but I ignored it and carried on as if I was still that naive 21-year-old who would do and say anything the promoter wanted them to do. I started to be plagued with countless injuries—broken bones, concussions, torn ligaments—but I refused to slow down. I wrestled, damn it, and nothing would stop me.

That wasn't the only price I paid.

I lost friends along the way. Ones who had been with me since day one, ones who had been with me through the highs and the lows. Wrestlers with whom I shared drinks and laughs died far too young, leaving holes in my life that no amount of filling could ever fill.

Drugs and alcohol. That's what we used back then to dull the pain and the depression we felt, and it cost us our families. It sure as hell cost me mine, and now, even all these years later, my own children won't even pick up the phone and call me.

But I didn't stop. I carried on, even on days when I could barely walk, but I saw things that I wish I had never seen. I saw things that no person should ever have to see. Wrestlers with broken backs and missing teeth, ones who could barely string a coherent sentence together when they had once been some of the most intelligent and well spoken people that I had ever met.

I saw people buckle under the weight of addictions too numerous to mention and the demons that came with them, which led me to be at so many funerals that I lost count. It was the dark side of the business that nobody had ever spoken about.

Still, I continued wrestling long after my glory days were behind me. I'd heard the mutterings, the rumours, and the jokes that I was becoming an embarrassment. Some even said that I was ruining what little legacy I had made for myself, but it didn't stop me. Even if I only managed to tag myself for two minutes of moves before having to tag out again, I was there. I didn't give a damn. I thought it was all I had left to offer.

Eventually, even my stubbornness was lost to the sheer amount of pain I was in daily, and the time came for me to announce my retirement.

Admitting that I just couldn't take it any more was one of the hardest things that I had ever had to do in my entire life. It broke my heart and left me feeling completely empty.

I remember stepping into the ring for the last time. I had stayed in the spotlight far too long, and it wasn't the farewell I'd imagined for myself, but still, the audience cheered and shouted for me as I struggled through the match. I was gasping for air after only a couple of minutes, but I knew I had to give them their money's worth, so I ignored the pain racing through me. It may have only been in front of about 60 or so people, but I treated it like I was in my heyday and it was in front of thousands.

It was the end of an era, my era, and as I look back on it now, I regret having stayed too long. I've heard there's footage of the match on the internet. I've even heard that some people watch it as a way of seeing what not to do in a match, but I don't care. Let them have their insults and their words; I've got my memories, and that's all I ever wanted to take away from my career.

I have to admit, it was hard to adjust to life outside the ring. For the first few years, I tried to silence that with bottle after bottle of whatever I could get my hands on. I'm dry now, as they say, and I don't regret that, but I do regret that it cost me so many of my friends and family. I didn't want to go down that route and be just another statistic on the list of dead professional wrestlers.

If anything, I felt lost without wrestling. It had been my life for so long that I wasn't sure what to do with myself now that it was gone.

Eventually, I found other things to occupy my time, especially after I got myself clean. I became a coach, helping to train the next generation of wrestlers at my school, hoping that they wouldn't make the same mistakes that so many of my generation made. I also started writing; hell, I've published several books about my career and life outside of the ring in the hopes that people would remember my name, my matches, and even some of the good things I did.

Now, as I sit on my porch, talking to you, I know it sounds like my career had its fair share of darkness, but I don't regret any of it. I made mistakes, ones I'm still learning from, but I'm still here when so many of my brothers and sisters in arms aren't.

I'm lucky, really. I know that. Hell, I even accept that.

Wrestling took everything from me, but it also gave me everything I've ever had. Life is funny that way, really.

The young man in front of me switched his recorder off and placed it in his pocket. He shook my hand happily and thanked me for the interview before leaving and making his way back to his car.

I watched as he slowly drove away, having spent the last couple of hours talking to them about my career. My name had started to be spoken of again as a contender for a place in the Memphis Wrestling Hall of Fame, but it was one of those things that I would believe when I saw it. I knew I had burned a lot of bridges there in my career, but it would be nice to be recognised for the good times there at least.

Leaning back, I felt proud of myself for telling my story and hoped, maybe vainly, that one of my children would read it and want to reach out to me. I'd tried many times over the years, but they hadn't wanted to know me—not that I could blame them for that.

Talking through my career, my hopes, my dreams, and my memories with the young reporter left me feeling a sense of contentment that I hadn't felt in decades. It was something I hadn't been sure about doing, but I was glad I'd relented and invited him over.

I was tired now, so I thought I deserved a nap before taking that afternoon's set of classes. Closing my eyes, I allowed myself the chance to dream of my life and of matches I'd had, and I smiled in my sleep.

Yes, wrestling has been my blood and my life force, and I wouldn't change it for the world.

Say Goodbye 'til it be Morrow

Adrian sat on the bed, lost in his own thoughts. Under him, the old mattress creaked slightly, with the springs feeling like they were trying to escape from the threadbare fabric.

The suit, the shirt, and the tie he was wearing felt constrictive, like a straitjacket, and he hated every second of it touching his body. Around him, the room looked disorganised but not messy. It was lived in, and he couldn't wait to be anywhere but here.

To his left, on the bedside cabinet, was a small photograph in an ornate, hand-carved frame. In it was a faded picture of Adrian with his arm around a woman, his wife, Amy. A smile was plastered on both of their faces as they stared out at whoever was looking at his back.

"It's going to be okay."

Adrian didn't look up, but he could see a pair of legs standing next to him and knew instantly who it was. Ignoring her, he played with his wedding ring, turning it around on his finger again and again. Amy took a step back and put her hands on her hips, a playful yet stern look crossing her kind face.

"Now, Adrian, you won't get much done sitting there, will you?"

Tears started to well up in Adrian's eyes as he turned his face slightly, as if to face her, while he still played with the ring on his finger. It felt comforting, but the sadness in the pit of his stomach pulsated.

"I can't do this. I just can't."

The way his shoulders slumped forward and the way he tried to make himself as small as possible made Adrian look like a frightened child in need of protection, so she slowly sat next to him. Taking another worried look at him, Amy placed her hand on his lower back and stroked it.

"Yes, you can. You can do anything. You're the bravest man I know; you always have been."

Adrian felt his whole body lunge forward violently, and he squeezed his hands into fists so tightly that his knuckles turned white from the pressure. He sniffed and swallowed hard, trying to stop the tears from running down his cheeks.

"I can't, I can't, I can't."

Reaching her hand out, Amy stroked the back of his head softly. She couldn't take her eyes away from him; the sadness was overwhelming him, and she felt helpless and unable to prevent it.

"I've got you; I've always got you, I promise."

Wrapping her arms around him, Amy knew that the only thing she could do was just hold him. It didn't take his sadness away, that was true, but it would at least let him know that she was there for as long as he needed her to be.

The sobs came hard and fast, taking over every facet of his thoughts and movements. The bed creaked and moved slightly under his weight as his entire body shook with the pain that had burst forth from him. In that moment, Adrian felt more lost than he had ever felt before.

After a few moments, Amy let go of him, stood up, and moved in front of his prone form. The way he shook and the sounds that came from him broke her heart, and she knelt in front of him, tears running from her eyes too. She wanted nothing more than to take his pain away and make him feel like the sun was shining and the day was going to be fine. Instead, she stroked his wet cheeks and just looked up at him.

"C'mon, Adrian. You're so much stronger than you know or give yourself credit for."

Standing up, Amy leaned over and took hold of the photo, smiling at their faces and beaming back at them. That was a good time, one of her favourites, and even now, it makes her smile.

"Do you remember that day, my love? Such a wonderful holiday, great weather, and some of the best food I've ever eaten."

Taking the frame in his hands, he pulled it closer and kissed it gently as he ran a finger around its edges.

"I remember that day. I asked you to marry me, then promptly fell flat on my face in the sand."

Putting the frame back on the bedside cabinet, he stood up and looked out of the window. The sun was shining outside, the weather couldn't be more perfect, and his daughter, Eden, was playing on the swing. He couldn't help but smile as she tried, with her grandfather's best push, to swing higher and higher.

Amy stepped behind him, wrapping her arms around his waist, and kissed him gently on the cheek before watching Eden too. There was such innocence in the girl's game, in the grin on her tiny little face, that, for the moment, all sadness was forgotten.

"You'll be okay, you know. I promise."

Outside, Eden saw that she was being watched and watched up at the window before making a look of pure concentration and trying to swing even higher than she already was, while her grandfather looked rather out of breath.

"I really can't do all of this. It's too much."

Turning away from the window so that Eden wouldn't see, Adrian felt the tears come once more, pushed down his cheeks by the growing panic that was making him feel light-headed. Amy watched with a look of concern on her face.

"You will be fine. I have way too much faith in you to think otherwise. Eden will be fine too. She's such a strong little thing."

As if a switch had been clicked, Eden had stopped playing and was now sitting sadly and talking to her grandfather. Leaning his back against the wall, Adrian looked up at the ceiling.

"Will I? Will she?"

Nothing Amy was saying seemed to be working or even having the slightest effect on her husband.

"You will. So will she."

He looked over at the photograph again and shook his head.

"You know, if my parents were here, they'd tell me to have faith. What a stupid thing to say. Have faith. In what? An imaginary person who apparently lives in the sky. How would that help anybody?"

The anger and bitterness in his words took Amy by surprise, and she took a step back, unsure of how to comfort him. She knew that his parents had been dead for over a decade, but there always seemed to be a darkness about their passing. It had affected him in so many ways, made it harder for him to trust anyone, and even convinced Adrian that it was only a matter of time before others were taken from him too. All because of the actions of a drunken idiot who decided to get behind the wheel of their car. Life had never been fair in that way to so many people; Adrian was just another one of them.

"Belief can help a lot of people. Just because it doesn't help you doesn't make it useless. Remember what you said to me when I lost my mother? Kindness is the best protection against pain. I always thought it was rather twee myself, but you know what? It worked."

"A man in the sky," laughed Adrian. "A fucking man in the sky."

He took another look out the window at Eden. This time his daughter was being embraced in a big, friendly hug. Amy rested her hand gently on his lower back and smiled.

"He always did love her to bits, didn't he? Dad always said that Eden was the one thing in his life that he had been missing since my mother died. I'm pretty sure that he even researched how to be a good grandfather to her; I wouldn't put it past him."

Amy wasn't sure if her words were helping Adrian or not, but she kept talking anyway.

"I promise, my love, she will be fine. She has my dad; she has you; what more could she want?"

She kissed his cheek and watched as he messed with the cuffs of his suit jacket, trying to make it more comfortable.

"It's time. You've got this. Be brave."

The sound of his father-in-law calling up the stairs made Adrian feel like a man walking down death row. Turning around, he saw the empty bedroom and sighed heavily before pulling the pamphlet from his pocket and heading towards the bedroom door. Closing it behind him, Adrian took a look at the golden-coloured font on the paper, its surface embossed with what looked like a butterfly wing design.

Just under a copy of the picture in the frame were six words, each one like a dagger to his chest.

In Loving Memory of Amy Oswald.

Words Like Blood

The ringing of the phone grew ever more insistent as its shrill tone danced around the room in vain, remaining unanswered by the man sitting in the armchair next to it with his brain and skull fragments decorating the wall behind him.

All around the room, there was an eerie sense of the macabre, an aura that only seemed to exist when a person had died.

That morning, everything had seemed so much brighter, hopeful even, as he had woken up, stretched, and made his way down stairs to make himself his customary cup of morning coffee. Jet black, five spoonfuls of sugar, as always. Just how he liked it.

Every day was the same. He would wake up, make the coffee, then head into the study to catch up on emails from his publisher, no doubt to give more excuses as to why he hadn't even begun to write the follow-up to his best-selling horror novel. He would then stare at the screen of his lap top, one with a very loud fan struggling to stop it from overheating, and watch as the cursor blinked in front of him.

Some days, but only some, he took the blinking, the empty screen, the lack of ideas, or even a single coherent sentence well. Other days, much like today, he wanted nothing more than to put his fist through the screen itself before picking up the phone and telling the publisher to go and fuck himself.

Oh, God. The publisher. He hated the young guy who had been put in charge of trying to wrangle some god-forsaken story out of his tired, old brain. At this point, he wasn't even sure that they even cared if the book was a good one. Hell, they would even be content to slap his hand on a turd and release it with a press release, calling it a work of art in the horror genre. What a load of absolute bollocks! It didn't help either that the lad was young enough to be his son. What made him think that he knew enough of the world to be able to get him to write a book that they could stick on the shelves of book stores hungry enough to sell anything with his name on it?

Looking up from the screen, he had taken a look at the plaques and awards that he had won for the book he'd released over three years ago.

The fans had gone completely bat-shit crazy for a story that was little more than a homage to the Stephen King stories that detailed a normal person's descent into madness and then murder. Well, he said homage, others said blatant rip-off, but to his publisher, they were one and the same. Then the plaudits, the awards, the interviews, even the mentions of his name, soon began to fade away and be forgotten. The promised movie adaptation of the novel fell by the wayside, and with it came the constant phone calls from the publisher asking where the next book was coming from.

Now, if anything, Paul was a blag artist of the highest order. He had to be; he was a writer, and he had to sell himself as better than any other so that people would sign him to a contract to do the one thing he used to love doing, writing. With that skill in hand, he'd managed to hold them at bay for a lot longer than he thought he would be able to do so. Then, when the plan started to fail, he just flat-out refused to answer the phone. That's when the damned emails started, slowly at first and then as a bombardment.

When each one appeared on screen, he just wanted to lose all sense and destroy every award and every single framed thing on the walls that even connected him to the book, no matter how small that link was.

With each passing day, the weight of expectation pushed him even further down into the seat in front of his desk. Even his wife had started to notice his posture and his body language changing into that of a lazy slouch. When she suggested that he take a break from his writing, something snapped in the back of his mind. It was no wonder that he couldn't get anything done. Distraction after distraction, nobody would just let him sit and work away on the next great American horror novel, but still the keys remained unpressed, the screen remained empty, and his mind remained full of regret that he'd ever written a book to begin with.

It's just writer's block. That's what he was told by friends, by his wife, and by his publisher, who, by now, had realised that he had done absolutely jack and shit by way of a follow-up novel. Just writers block. Three simple words that made it sound painfully simple yet really fucking insulting at the same time. If it really was that easy, then he would have been a millionaire by now, churning out book after book and just slapping his name on the cover, no matter the quality of the words inside. It seemed to work for other authors, so why not him?

But no, it wasn't that simple. Here he was, sat in his chair, laptop on and its screen casting a pallid glow on his already pale skin, and feeling unable to even write the shortest of coherent sentences.

For the first time that day, the phone began to ring. He hated that shrill, high-pitched tone, but he loved sticking his middle finger up towards it in mock salute.

As always, as soon as the phone began to ring, Pamela shouted down to him to kindly let him know that it was indeed ringing, as if he hadn't already noticed it. Shaking his head, he called back to say thank you, then went right back to ignoring the annoying little shit of a phone.

On the screen in front of him, without realising it, he'd written two words over and over. Some were indented on the left, others on the right, and a few lines were even dead centre.

Fuck off.

Admittedly, it wasn't his best writing; it would barely crack into his personal top ten, but it was better than anything he'd managed to write recently.

Keep fucking off.

Nope. That was overkill. The young idiot at his publisher, the one who thought he knew it all, kept telling him that he needed to be edited more, to use fewer words, and this was his personal favourite of all the constructive criticism: to use less flowery language.

Fuck off.

Yes, that was better. Stick to the classics, Paul. Stick to the classics.

Leaning back in the chair, he let out a loud sigh, added a few choice curse words, and then cracked his knuckles. A few taps of the keys later, and a couple of sentences on the screen appeared before he furiously jabbed at the backspace button, deleting them as if they were some dirty secret to never be seen again.

Flicking through the open tabs on his laptop screen, he saw there were seven new emails from his publisher, one with "BLOODY READ THIS ONE, PAUL!" as its subject matter. He clicked on it, sent the email into the spam folder, and smirked, knowing that it was going to annoy the ever-loving hell out of the prick who had sent it.

Clicking back to the screen where his story should be, Paul stared and watched it blink. At first, he started to count each flash of the cursor but felt his eyes grow heavier with each movement. Before he knew it, he'd lost track of a couple of hours. It was the first time that he'd gotten even the tiniest amount of sleep in so long that he couldn't remember. He couldn't remember when the last time he bathed was either. Not that it mattered; it wasn't like he was going to be going anywhere any time soon. Not while he had this fucking book to write.

The sound of someone slightly knocking on the door made him jolt in the chair. Startled, Paul looked towards the door, his heart pounding in his chest. Who could it be? He wasn't expecting anyone, and anyone who would come to see him knew better than to do so when he was writing. They knew the rules. He'd told them often enough.

With a deep and heavy sigh, he pushed himself out of the chair and trudged towards the door. He knew, deep down, that it would be easier to just be kind to whoever was on the other side because then, more than anything, they would leave quickly and quietly.

As he opened it, he was met with the concerned gaze of Mrs. Murphy, their neighbour, a gossip hound, and a talented baker too. She was a sweet older lady who sometimes brought biscuits and cakes around to them whenever he was deep in work, or at least what he told them was work.

"Paul, my dear, are you alright?" She asked, and, for the first time since he'd met her years ago, he noticed the deep worry lines on her face.

"I'm fine, Mrs. Murphy. Just really busy writing my next magnum opus," he lied. If there was one thing he didn't want to do, it was keep her here longer than he absolutely had to. He'd always thought when people told him that misery loved company that it was complete and utter bullshit. He just wanted to be left the fuck alone.

"I'd not seen you for days, and your lovely wife let me in. She said something about me being able to talk some sense into you about this story, but, you know me, I don't like to interfere."

Now Paul knew only too well that her words were little more than lies. She loved to hide behind her curtains, watching people come and go, in the hopes that she would hear some kind of gossip that she could then spread around herself.

"I'm fine; honestly, I am. I've just got to write this stupid book and get it sent off to the publisher. That's all."

The look that crossed Mrs. Murphy's face was more than clear enough to show Paul that she didn't believe him, but he gave her one back of his own, with the message that he wanted her to leave right now.

Closing the door behind him once more, not giving her the chance to say goodbye or to change her mind and complain about whatever was bothering her that day, he couldn't shake the feeling that he was a failure in all he did. He couldn't write a simple thing as a sequel to a horror book; he was a failure as a husband and even as a simple human being. He was the reverse of King Midas in all things. Everything he touched turned to shit.

Returning to the study, with its comfortable armchair and not-so-comfortable office chair, he stared at the blinking cursor once more. His mind was a jumbled mess of ideas, of lines of dialogue, even of death scenes, but they mixed with the frustration and self-doubt that plagued him. Writers block. A simple name for something that was intent on keeping him prisoner in his own mind as well as his own study.

The phone rang again, its shrill and annoying tone cutting through the silence of the room. Paul glared at it, anger welling up from deep inside him. Within seconds, he had snatched up the phone and hurled it across the room, watching as it crashed against the wall, shattering into too many pieces for him to count.

Breathing heavily, he surveyed the damage that he had caused. Two of the framed awards had fallen to the floor, along with one of the statues. He'd always hated those ugly things and only kept them as proof that he had actually achieved something in his life, even if it was little more than a story written by a hack like him. For a moment, he felt a sense of twisted satisfaction in having broken something, but it quickly subsided, leaving only emptiness in its wake.

Suddenly an idea burst into his mind, one so twisted, so fucked up, that it would only make sense if it was put into a book written by someone like him, someone who had written a horror novel before, one that even Stephen King himself had described as "readable," which was still the best thing he'd read about his work. He was going to channel his anger and frustration into this story, and it was going to work. It was going to get the publisher off his back, and some money was rolling into his pockets at last.

"Pamela, can you come here for a moment?"

***

Grabbing a notepad and a pen, he scribbled the words furiously onto the paper. He was done with the expectations, the pressure, and the constant reminders of his past solitary success. It was time to create something that was truly his own, something that would only ever be connected to his name, unburdened by opinions and demands by those who should have known better.

As he scribbled the words, each line flowed from him like a dam bursting, flooding the pages with his pent-up creativity. He wrote about anguish, despair, loneliness, and all that had threatened to consume him. It was raw, unfiltered, and unlike anything he had created before.

Hours turned into days as Paul put everything he had into his work. He didn't notice the passing of time, nor did it matter much to him either. The one thing that did matter was the story he was weaving, one that reflected everything he had felt. The scratching of the pen on the paper had replaced the tapping of the keyboard, and it fuelled his body as his hands moved across the pages quicker than before.

As the days turned into weeks and the smells that had been hiding in the shadows were now wrapping themselves around him like a rotten vine, he wrote the final sentence and dropped the notepad onto the desk. Slumping deeper into the chair, exhausted but relieved. The manuscript lay before him, a testament to his broken mind and his creativity.

Snatching the pad back up, he had the all-consuming desire to read it. Flicking through the pages, he couldn't help but think he had written a masterpiece, something that would finally shut that young idiot up and get something new with his name emblazoned on the cover on the book shelves.

Filled with a renewed sense of pride and purpose, Paul started to tap out an email to the publisher, one full of hyperbole, but he didn't care. There was no trace of hesitation or even humbleness as he confidently told them that he had written the next great American masterpiece.

Days passed with no reply, and the old, familiar feelings of failure began to feel all-encompassing. The dimly lit room started to feel like it was closing in on him.

"Pamela, I did it. I wrote the best book I've ever read. I did it. Look."

Walking over to her, Paul waved the notepad in front of her face, growing ever more frustrated when she didn't answer him. Dropping it into her lap, he looked down for the first time and saw they were dirty, ink-stained, and had dried blood flaking from them. That's when he noticed it. Her once-vibrant eyes were lifeless as they stared back at him, her pale neck now trisected by a deep, angry gash.

As the torment and the realisation of what he had really done pulled and stabbed at his sense of reality, her glassy eyes stared at him forever more. Shadows twisted and danced on the walls, whispering grotesque secrets into his ear. They taunted him with the promises he had made to Pamela—to provide her with a good home, safety, and a family—but now she lay dead in his study, his manuscript left on her lap.

In the confined space, with only his dead wife for company, Paul's grip on reality slowly started to unravel even more. His mind spun intricate webs of elaborate fantasies in which Pamela still lived, with visions of a life so deliriously happy that in those moments, all was forgotten. The solace the visions brought to him was only temporary, the merciless truth shattering the illusions that his mind so sorely wanted him to believe in.

Quickly, shocking even himself, Paul became a shell of himself, turning into a haggard, dishevelled shadow of a man. Hollow eyes stared back at him, full of regret and pain, leaving him to see only a stranger who had destroyed everything that he had found dear in his life.

Convinced that Pamela's spirit lived on in the walls of the study, Paul became afraid to leave the room, scared that she would escape and leave him alone forever-more. Still, her voice caressed his ears, telling him that this was his doing, that this was his fault, and he knew that. The accusatory tone she used only served to tell him what he already knew—that he had killed her.

It was in the moonlit hours that the voices became harsher and more aggressive in how they spoke to him. Nightmares had merged with reality, the imagined becoming the reality.

As the first light of that morning's dawn cracked through the dirty windows, bathing him in light and a strange warmth, he knew what he needed to do.

Sitting in the armchair and looking directly at Pamela staring back at him with blank, lifeless eyes, he placed the muzzle of the gun in his mouth before closing his eyes and pulling the trigger—his last act in this world.

Once the gunshot had faded, its echo lost in the fibres of the study, another noise took over, one that had been the bane of his existence. The sound of a telephone ringing, the mobile locked in his draw vibrating with each ring, only to go forever unanswered.

Lily

In the tiny town of Sweetbrook, a quiet and old-fashioned place if ever there was one, stood a house full of rumours, mysteries, and even horror stories.

Some spoke of a supernatural creature that resided in the house, surrounded by the four walls that struggled to hold it up. It had stood abandoned for decades, with nobody even wanting to go near it, let alone live there, and because of that, the story of the creature grew and grew. The now dirty and broken windows that were once so vibrant were near impossible to look through, if anyone was brave enough to do so.

Others spoke of it being haunted by the spirit of its previous owner, who committed suicide after being jilted by a past lover. There was no evidence of that ever happening, but, with Sweetbrook being such a small and rather boring place, they weren't going to let facts stand in the way of a good story like that, especially one with tragically romantic undertones like that.

To some, thanks to some children seemingly investigating the place for themselves long ago, a story of music emanating from the house became popular too. It was said, thanks to the children's over-active imaginations, that the music was the only remnant of a once-happy life that had lived inside. It was also said that they had seen a ghostly apparition dancing inside, but with each retelling, the ghost changed. Soon, just like the building that had inspired it, the story grew old and forgotten.

The music, however, remained. Was it imagination, or was it a trick of the mind? There was no answer. Like most things, it was just there, winding its way through the fog and mist that had made the grounds around the house their home.

However, on this night, a Halloween night of all things, Lily had other ideas. She had heard the stories; she had heard whispered rumours of ghosts and spirits, and it had excited her more than anything, so on went her costume, on went her boots, and she set off to investigate.

Now, Lily was a child that was seen as rather strange and unusual by the other children in Sweetbrook. She always had her head buried deeply in whatever book she could find in the tiny library in town and read it from cover to cover. It didn't matter what the book was; she just had an insatiable need and desire to read as many of them as she could.

This night was no different.

Inside her backpack, which she was pretty sure was held together by the dozens of badges she had attached to it, all of which were as varied as the books she read, was a well-read copy of The Lord of the Rings. She'd read it before, twice in fact, but when the library was so small, she knew she had to appreciate any title she could get from there. Her costume, one she had made herself, left her looking like a character from the very same book, complete with papier-mâché elf ears, although those were a mistake considering the rainy weather.

Another thing that Lily liked to do, which was yet another thing that the other children found weird, was play the guitar. She was good too, with an uncanny ability to hear a song once, especially if it was a classic rock song played on her father's record player, and be able to learn the riffs and solos that her heroes played.

Now the idea of a house where mysterious music lived was something that had done far more than pique a child's innocent sense of adventure. It had made her determined to discover if the stories were true or if it was just really an empty house that was ready to be torn down by those who ran the town. Well, ready to be torn down if they could make their minds up and all vote together without arguing amongst themselves.

One of the stories that she'd heard other children speak about, when they thought she was too busy reading to hear what they were saying, was about a guitar inside the house. It wasn't just any old guitar either; they said it was a cursed instrument, one that would play the saddest chords to make even the coldest heart break. She didn't believe it; she was 12 after all and not prone to flights of fancy, thank you very much, but there was just something that told her she needed to see it for herself.

In her mind, she hoped it was somewhat true. She could take the guitar, harness its ability, and write a song so popular that it would mean she and her dad could find somewhere better to live than a town that was barely holding itself together.

After a short walk through the trees, Lily found herself standing at the gate to the house. The garden was overgrown, the weeds had clearly taken over, and the house itself looked so wrecked that it took on the appearance of a building made from wet, dirty cardboard and not bricks and mortar. The way everything looked sparked her brain into action, and she tried to imagine who could have lived in a place like this. Had it been a tortured musician, a jilted lover, maybe even a dangerous criminal? She didn't know; nobody did, and that was what made the place so irresistible to her.

With so many weeds and plants snatching at her ankles, Lily struggled to walk up to the door of the house, taking great pride in using the curse words she knew but wasn't allowed to use at home.

The closer she came to the front door, the more the smell of wet mould seemed to want to push her away. The aroma was disgusting, clinging to her nostrils and making her want to gag, but she'd come this far, and an unpleasant smell wasn't going to be the thing that made her turn back and go home.

Pushing the door open and feeling a sharp pang of surprise that it wasn't locked, Lily stepped inside and sighed. The house may have been a wreck; it may look like it hadn't had a good clean in decades, but at least she was now out of the rain, something that her now-drooping handmade elf ears were more than grateful for.

As she looked around, Lily was surprised at how small the rooms were. The building wasn't exactly big, but some of the rooms inside were so small that she was able to stretch out her arms and touch the walls with her hands. They looked badly put together, as if they had been added by someone who'd read a how-to article on the internet and then given it a go themselves. Shaking her head and grinning excitedly as the floorboards creaked in time with her footsteps, she made her way to the next room.

A beautiful musical chord seemed to drift throughout the house, but Lily wondered if it was just her mind playing tricks on her after hearing so many stories about this place. The teachers at the school had always told her that she would lose herself in the stories she heard or read, but she didn't see that as a bad thing. The world around her wasn't kind; it was hard and sometimes cruel, so if losing herself in a good story helped her cope, then where was the problem? It was no different here. She was just lost in the story. That's all it was, but even then, even with that knowledge, she wanted to follow the sound back to its source, whether it was real or not.

Making her way up the dirty, dust-covered stairs, the music became louder, and Lily smiled. Yes, she was lost in this story, and she was going to enjoy every moment of it before going back home to tell her father all about the things she had seen.

A glint caught her eye, and she looked up, seeing a small length of rope hanging down from the ceiling with a small metal ring tied to the end of it. Reaching out, she really wanted to pull it and see what happened next, but she remembered something her father always used to say. Be curious, but not so curious as to fall into stupidity. Taking a deep breath, she shrugged, counted to ten, and then gave the ring a sharp pull.

Lily let out a squeal of excitement as, a second or two after a loud clicking sound, a set of stairs descended, stopping right in front of her and no doubt leading to an attic. They looked out of place compared to the rest of the house, even managing to look clean and well-maintained.

"C'mon, girl, explore. That's what you're here for. Get up those stairs and look some more."

Laughing at her attempt to rap, she took her first tentative step onto the first stair in front of her. It seemed to hold her weight without creaking or threatening to fall apart, giving her a quick boost of confidence before she rushed up the rest of them, finding herself standing inside an attic full to the brim with boxes, paintings, and all sorts of things that reminded her of treasure in the old movies her father liked so much.

Leaning against a large but decaying chair, which somehow still managed to look like it would be comfortable to sit in, stood the thing she was looking for. An old, weathered guitar. Punching the air, she stepped towards it, wanting to snatch the instrument up and rush home with it.

Kneeling down, Lily couldn't help but stare at the guitar. It was impossible to take her eyes away from it. She was sure that the strings vibrated with an energy she couldn't explain. It was as if they were promising the most beautiful song and the most beautiful sounds that she could ever hear.

A melody emanated from the strings, one that enticed her, and she snatched up the guitar, holding it close to her chest. It was like a siren's call, and she didn't want to put it down. In her mind, this guitar was hers now and hers alone.

The wooden body felt cold against her chest, and the strings even more so against the tips of her fingers as she tried to decide whether to pluck them or not. A quiet whispering sound surrounded her, despite her being alone in the attic, and her fingers twitched, eager to play the instrument for the first time in decades.

As soon as her fingers plucked the first chord, the energy moved from the music into her. It was like electricity had been shocked through her veins, and she stood up, playing louder and faster than she had ever thought possible. Her playing became effortless and skilled beyond any measure she had ever known. Melodies flowed from her fingertips, captivating and motivating her in equal measure. It was like the guitar was either playing itself or controlling her every movement.

Time had no power or hold over her here. Minutes turned into hours. Hours turned into days. Days turned into weeks. If anyone was looking for her, then she didn't know about it, nor did she care.

Lily immersed herself in the guitar's power, and soon, the outside world and the people in it were forgotten.

Unbeknownst to her, the people of Sweetbrook had been looking for her, while her broken-hearted father blamed himself for her disappearance. It was like a clichéd crime drama—the low-to-no, budget thing you saw on the internet.

The authorities had, of course, looked into the father first. It was, after all, statistically a family member that would do home to a child first and foremost, but he was quickly written off as a suspect in her disappearance. It didn't stop the rumours, and he soon retreated back into his home, only coming out to get the essentials.

Some told tall tales of the haunted house having taken her. Nobody believed them. The few people that did, despite their best efforts, couldn't find the house, no matter how long they looked for.

Lily, on the other hand, didn't care. She didn't even know, and as the days and weeks passed, her youthful appearance disappeared, replaced by dark circles under her eyes and a haunted look on her face. She didn't sleep or eat, as her hair turned to pure white while she played the chords.

Whispers spread throughout Sweetbrook once more. Stories of a haunted house holding the soul of a once happy, intelligent child within its walls, leaving only an old lady in her place.

Rumours abounded of music once more coming from inside, and still, the children of the town wanted to explore the building that had given birth to the ghost stories their parents told them every Halloween night.

Years passed; the children grew into adults and had children of their own, sharing the stories with them too. Each time the tale of Lily was told, it grew more and more outrageous. One even said that she flew around the town on a broom, playing a guitar, to entice all the naughty children of the town to the house. Despite no children going missing, the story itself still took on a life of its own.

One night, decades after Lily had disappeared and after her father had been long dead and buried, a group of townsfolk met and took a vote. It was time, if they could find it, to leave the house as a pile of rubble, and that was that, but they were a superstitious bunch now. The stories, long told as a way to keep the children in line and convince them to behave, had gnawed under their skin and twisted their minds. The house had to be demolished, and they didn't care how.

Under the cover of darkness, they trooped through the woods and through the trees, astounded that they seemed to know where the house was after all these years.

Stopping, with their hands full of holy water in old coke bottles, blessed by the local priest, crucifixes, and even a burning desire to pull the place down brick by brick.

As they walked, they whispered stories of Lily and her condition, some even saying that a witch had cursed her to walk the woods alone, the cursed guitar strapped to her back. When it was said out loud, they knew it sounded stupid, that it sounded childish in its simplicity, but still they marched on until they came to the house itself.

Standing proudly in front of them, the first thing they noticed was that it had changed. The windows were no longer cracked. The garden was well kept and tended to. If anything, it now looked like a home, albeit one that an amateur builder was trying to keep together at all costs.

Another thing that made no sense was the simple fact that, after years of looking, they had found it. Trip after trip to the forest had come up empty-handed, but now it wanted to be found.

The group felt a need to open the door and rush in, rescuing Lily in the process, pulling her away from the curse, and maybe even giving her back her life. That's not what they found inside.

As they kicked the door in, running up the stairs and into the attic, they found the place completely empty, save for a polished, well-kept guitar leaning against the wall, its strings forever still.

No matter where they looked, Lily was nowhere to be found. It was as if she had vanished into thin air, never to be seen again, but left in her stead were the ghostly echoes of a lingering melody, haunting those brave enough to listen and take heed of its warnings.

The stories of Lily's disappearance changed, merging into a moral story, one warning of chasing curses in the name of betterment. It became somewhat of a legend told amongst the townsfolk, a myth to entertain and chill the blood of the little ones who still believed in magic. It became a tale of how, if you listened carefully on a stormy night, just like any other good ghost story, you could hear the sound of Lily's tormented music playing and being carried through the wind.

For now, however, the guitar lays dormant, waiting for its next victim to pick it up, fall into its spell, and play the chords that would make the player's soul its own, leaving them forever destined to play the chords of the damned.

Long Time Listener, First Time Caller

Daniel George.

To most, it was a name that didn't sound special or particularly memorable. He could walk past you in the street, and you wouldn't bat an eye.

To the listeners of his late-night radio show, he was like a god of the airwaves, a man known for taking an unknown band or an unknown song and making it a known best seller and sending it to the top of the charts.

Most nights, he would drive to the radio station with his trusty bottle of Jack Daniels in the glove compartment, ready to take calls, play music, and generally say whatever he knew he could get away with.

It was the same routine every single night, and he wouldn't change it for the world. He loved the fans he had, and there were a lot of them who listened to his show religiously. He loved the music he played; it was his entire life.

Tonight was no different. Gary stepped out of the car and looked at the building with a smile on his well-lined face. It wasn't much to look at; in fact, it looked like a run-down place ready to be demolished, but he looked at it as a home of sorts. It was somewhere he could let loose, somewhere he could say whatever he wanted, and somewhere he was the king of the radio.

He had been the DJ of Chanson City Radio's late-night show for the last 25 years. Of course he had been offered better time slots; he had even been offered contracts for other stations that would have left him never wanting for money again. He turned them all down without a second thought.

Some would have said he was set in his ways, that he was stagnant, stuck in a rut, or maybe that he was even a dinosaur waiting for the comet that would end everything. He, on the other hand, was just the simplest of things. He was happy.

Walking into the building and nodding a quick hello to the elderly security guard who had been there for even longer than he had, he made his way to the small room that held the equipment—the microphones—that he saw as the golden tools of his trade.

The bottle clinked as he placed it next to the battered, old microphone that he refused to get replaced. It was his lucky charm—the thing that he saw as his reason for success.

A clock above him ticked as he waited for his show to start. He knew that his assistant was working away in the next room, making sure that the transition between shows was as smooth as silk. He didn't even have to look up and check; the man knew how to do his job blindfolded. If anything, his time management was so good that Daniel had never seen the DJ who hosted the show before him. They were like ships in the night, never meant to meet, and he liked it that way. It kept his mind sharp and ready to make that night's show the best that he could.

The lights on the equipment began to flash, telling him that he had thirty seconds before it would all begin.

Almost in the blink of an eye, the show was live, and Daniel launched into his normal, well-rehearsed spiel, one he knew by heart.

"Hello, and welcome to the Twilight World of Daniel George, and tonight, oh boy, we have a show and a half for you."

Taking the briefest of glances, Daniel saw his assistant give his customary thumbs-up signal to say that they already had callers.

"Well, it looks like some of you are certainly excited to talk to me tonight. All I can assume is that some of you have daddy issues and want to spend your evenings talking to a washed-up shock jock like me—not that I mind. My face does make a good replacement for a seat, or so I've been told."

Daniel didn't need to look up; he knew that his assistant would be laughing. He was just playing a character; okay, it was an extension of himself, but when he was on air, it was easy to be someone else and to throw his inhibitions in the trash can, even if only for a couple of hours.

"Later tonight, we will be speaking to the latest viral sensation, a man who, for some unknown reason, keeps filming himself jumping off of things while dressed as a third-rate superhero, but first, oh yes, let's hear your sexy voices."

Looking over at the switchboard, he saw that, once again, the damn thing wasn't working and raised an eyebrow. His assistant, Terry, shrugged and looked nonplussed.

"Well, it's a lucky dip. The screen isn't working, so now is your chance to be whoever you want to be. Surprise me; make me moist; make me nice and sweaty with excitement."

There was an excited noise on the line, and Daniel rolled his eyes. It would be another drunken teenager, no doubt, on their way home after getting wasted with their friends. While those sorts of calls are what brought the viewers in with their drunken jokes and the idea that anything could and would happen, he hated them. They bored him; it took too long to get them to hang up; and, if he was being completely honest with himself, they reminded him too much of when he would get drunk and forget whole chunks of time. If there was one thing he didn't like, it was random drunken idiots holding up a mirror to him and showing just what he became when drinking.

"First time caller, long time listener," said the caller, a young-sounding female voice that then quickly descended into a fit of giggles before talking again. "Like, oh my god, that was so cringe-worthy, right? But I have, like, a question for you."

Daniel rubbed his eyes roughly, took a swig from his bottle, and then leaned closer to the mic. "Are you even old enough to be up this late? Don't you have homework to do?"

There it was—another burst of giggling as the caller tried her best to sound flirty in her drunken state.

"Oh, Daniel, you make me laugh."

"Yeah, well, that's kind of my job. I'm here to talk, be funny, and play records. Now, what is your question? Make it a good one."

"I know you're, like, old and stuff, but is it true that old guys are better in bed?"

As soon as she asked the question, there was an absolute explosion of laughter. She was clearly with a group of friends, and this was a prank call, but he knew what to do and what his listeners expected. Filth, and he was ready to unleash it.

"Well, you know where the studio is. Come find out. Hell, come sit on my lap, and I'll pretend to be Santa."

The line went dead, silencing the raucous, high-pitched laughter, and Daniel felt almost relieved to be rid of the caller. This was starting to get boring. What happened to the good old days, when, in addition to deliberately trying to shock people and get a reaction, there was a good mix of callers? Some even asked for his advice on things like movies and music.

Shrugging, he pressed the button again and waited for the next caller to speak, hoping that this one would be more interesting than the last. Taking a deep breath, he prepared himself to be in character.

"You are through to Daniel George, the silver fox with the golden cock. If your question is about my genitalia, then it's large and in charge; you're on the air."

"You're a real piece of shit, Daniel. You know that, right?"

He looked up at Terry, who was lost in a book, and swore under his breath. As bored as the guy was, he was meant to screen the calls. Ones like this one did nothing for the listeners; hell, they made them switch off.

"Well, thank you. I love you too."

Hanging up, Daniel noticed that the lights were out, leaving him confused. They had all been blinking only moments before, creating a wall of flashing lights for him to answer.

This time, Terry was paying attention but shrugged and tapped at his earpiece to say it was working fine.

"Well, we appear to have lost that wonderfully well-spoken caller. What a shame that is. Now, onto the first song of the evening. An oldie but one of the good ones. Listeners, this is 'People Are Strange' by The Doors."

Taking his headset off as the song began, Daniel took a deep breath and looked up at Terry.

"Terry, my man, what the fuck was that? You have one job, and not only did you let someone on air to insult, but we've lost all the callers, not just him. What the actual fuck, Terry?"

"I didn't do shit. The phone lines went down. I'm not the technician; I'm just here to make sure you don't get us sued, you daft old bastard."

Daniel laughed quietly as Terry looked offended before going back to reading his book, a thriller by James Patterson. Placing his headset back on, he felt proud of himself, as he had timed it perfectly with the ending of the song.

"Well, that was a bit of a good one, wasn't it? In other news, we appear to have lost our callers due to a technical hitch, but hey, it happens. This place is falling down around us, so I'm not surprised. Even Jesus would look at this stuff and tell us it's old."

One of the lights flashed slowly, and Daniel smiled.

"Well, well, well. It looks like we have another caller. Welcome to my show, where we talk music, movies, dicks, and more. Speak or forever hold my piece."

"You are a real piece of shit. You deserve all the shit that karma is going to shove down your throat. I hope you choke on it, really, I do."

Great, just great. Out of all the callers who managed to fight their way through the technical issues, it had to be this one.

Looking up at Terry, Daniel could see that he was already prepared for what he was going to say. A piece of torn cardboard was held up against the glass with the words "Speak to him; he's the only caller we have!" written hastily on it.

Rolling his eyes, Daniel took another deep breath and spoke.

"I'm guessing, my friend, that you're having a bit of a bad day. Why not tell us about it?"

He'd tried his best to sound concerned, to sound like he cared, but it was clear to anyone listening that he didn't.

"You know about it already, Daniel. You know who I am. Look at the damned screen. It will tell you the number I'm calling from."

Glancing at the screen, he recognised the number immediately and felt his stomach tighten. He had to get rid of his phone call and this person as quickly as he could. This was his show; how dare this idiot try to phone in and take over?

"You ruined my life. You took everything from me. And look at you now. You have the money, the house, the car, and even your own radio show, but you're too damn cheap to update the place. I doubt the others even know you own the fucking building you work in."

Terry looked up from his book with a surprised look on his face, but Daniel waved it away dismissively.

"I'm going to be honest; I don't even know who you are," he replied, knowing straight away that he shouldn't have said it.

"Now, you've not changed. You're still as bad a liar as you've always been."

That was it; he'd had enough. Ending the call, he pressed another button and played the next song without saying a word. This time, it was a song called 'Weak' by Skunk Anansie, but it felt strangely out of place in the aftermath of the call.

As the song reached its crescendo, another light flashed in front of Daniel, this time with a different phone number, and he found himself smiling. The call had freaked him out and gotten under his skin, and he was glad it was over.

"And we are back, my dear listeners. I hope I didn't leave you with blue balls with that disappearance, but hey, at least I left you with a great song. Now we have another caller. Hopefully this one is happier to speak to me, eh?"

"You hung up on me; that was rude, don't you think?"

That voice. It was him again.

"And do you think I would honestly make it that easy for you to get rid of me?"

"Fine. Pray tell. What am I, a mere DJ, meant to have done to you to ruin your life? Did I fuck your girlfriend, your mom, or your dad? Shit, did I fuck your dog? What? What did I do?"

Daniel looked up and felt a surge of anger as Terry looked back at him with a thumbs up, mouthing that the phone call was "some good shit" and to carry on.

"Do you think it was really that simple? I'd be doing this because you fucked someone I know? Don't be so pathetically clichéd."

There was no need to reply; Daniel even doubted that there was anything he could say in any way, so he snatched his bottle and took another swig.

"I'm not even there, and I can already tell you're drinking. What even are you? Did you read "Tortured Soul 101" and copy it word for word?"

"Oh, fuck you. You called me, not the other way around. What do you want? This is my show. MY SHOW!"

Again, Terry was ecstatically sticking his thumb up to encourage him, but Daniel threw the bottle at the window, making it smash and spill Jack Daniels everywhere and leaving a dark mark on the window in front of his assistant. It only took a moment for him to throw his earphones down and walk out, leaving Daniel on his own.

"I heard that. Temper, temper, Mr. George. You're not exactly setting a good example for your listeners, are you?"

For a moment, the air was silent. Listeners would no doubt be looking on in confusion, wondering just what was happening on tonight's show.

"Dead air. That's not a good thing for a DJ, you know. I would have thought with all your experience that you would have known that."

"Fuck off. Hang up and let me do my job."

More laughter. This time it wasn't from a drunken, horny girl. It was from someone who seemed intent on ruining the show.

"Hang up, or I will do it for you."

"No, no, you won't. Not if you know what's good for you. Now the police have been notified that there will be an incident here tonight, on this very show. The funny thing is, they didn't believe me. Something about you making prank calls, fake reports, and the like. They did, however, tell me to go fuck myself, albeit in your name."

"You son of a bitch."

"That's quite funny you should say that, Daniel. That's what they called you, too. Now, where were we?"

Daniel slammed his hand down on the desk, swearing loud enough for the mic to pick it up.

"Well, you appear to be shooting your load in your underwear about insulting me. So, shoot your shot, clean yourself up, and let me get on with playing some music."

"Oh, if only it were that simple, my friend," the voice replied mockingly. "You know me; I know you; but your listeners don't. So, with that in mind, I vote that we begin a bit of story time. I really hope your listeners are sitting comfortably."

Pushing himself away from the microphone, Daniel began to pace up and down the small room. It didn't take long—only a few steps—but it didn't help either. He just felt trapped, and no matter how many times he stared at the door, he couldn't bring himself to leave.

"Look," he said, feeling the knot in his stomach grow even tighter, "I'm sorry that I hurt you in any way. I truly am, but you have to believe me that it wouldn't have been anything intentional."

"Oh, don't brush me off like that. You're better than that. Even an immoral, disgusting thing like you is better than that."

The sanctimonious, "holier than thou" attitude of the caller was making Daniel feel even more panicked. He could remember the number it was coming from and the face of the person calling, but the one thing he couldn't remember was just what he had done to apparently deserve this.

He wasn't naive. He was a shock jock, although he hated that term with a passion, and he had hurt people to get where he was today. His wife had left him, neither of his children wanted anything to do with him, and he was just one more thing away from having won "cliché bingo," and he had smashed that when he threw the bottle at Terry.

"Now, be a good boy and listen to me, Daniel. You will hear my story, they will hear my story, and then all of this will end, but only then. This needs to be heard; you need to be held accountable for your own actions like an adult should be."

He nodded, agreeing with what he was hearing. It was true; he should be held accountable for his actions, but the problem with that was that he had done so many things wrong that he didn't know where to start. The one thing—the only thing—he was sure of was that there would be no redemption waiting for him at the end of all of this.

"I take your silence, Mr. Shock Jock, as permission to continue, so I shall."

There was a click of a tape player, and some muffled music played over the phone line before stopping.

"Sorry, I couldn't resist it. I wanted my own theme music, although I suppose I could have just used yours. You won't be needing it after this."

"Just get on with it; tell me and tell them what I am supposed to have done to you. They're listening; I'm listening, so come on. What's the story you are so eager to tell? This isn't "Story Time with Mommy," nor is it an open mic night at a nearby pub."

"Patience, patience, old man. It's not like you have anywhere to go."

Daniel rushed over to the door, full of a sudden compulsion to leave and never come back to this place. The door rattled as he tried to open it. Someone had locked it from the outside.

"Told you. Don't try to kick it open either; there are some things that you just can't fix with brute force, although, lord knows, you will try."

Despite what the voice said, he tried kicking the door any way he could. The only thing that succeeded in doing was hurting his foot, and he swore again and limped up and down the room.

"I heard that, and, to be fair, I did warn you. Now, sit your old ass down and listen. That goes for your listeners too. They're about to bear witness to the downfall of their idol, an old drunk who plays music for a living."

Daniel let himself flop down into his chair and tried to ignore the pain in his leg. He still couldn't remember who this person was or what he had done wrong, but his mind played a thousand different scenarios in his head.

He'd had affair after affair, allowing the fans to come to him and offering them anything they wanted in exchange for him getting laid. Daniel never kept any of those promises, nor had he ever intended to, but they were foolish and easily convinced.

His wife had left him, taking the children with her, leaving him to be yet another story of a drunk with an attitude problem who had nobody to care for him.

Before tonight, it hadn't bothered him, or if it had, it was drowned under the drinks he poured down his gullet.

Bribes. That was another thing he had taken part in. It was so easy. A wad of cash here, a wad of cash there, and he had his own radio show that didn't have to adhere to any of the rules and regulations.

That was the good thing about having money. It could get you out of anything you found yourself in. DUI charges, gone. Speeding tickets, gone. Loneliness, just pay for some companionship, and that was gone too.

He had never thought of himself as some paragon of virtue; he hadn't even thought of himself as a good man. Instead, Daniel just found himself muddling through life and ignoring any of the mess he left in his wake.

"Daniel George is not, was not, and never has been a good person. He would use you, chew you up, spit you out, and every other type of stereotype you can imagine. He wasn't even particularly original in his approach to life either: If you were useful, then he was on your side; if you weren't, then he would destroy you."

He could feel himself spiralling downward, his thoughts threatening to bring him down with no way for him to get back up. All he could do was let the words wash over him on their way to drown his sorry, drunken ass.

"I was someone who was never on his side. I had no reason to be. He made me promises; he told me my songs were going to be the biggest hits he had ever heard. I was young, I was naive, and, well, I was stupid. So, no, I wasn't on his side, but I was under his spell, like the others he had left by the wayside. I did everything he said, even when I didn't want to. I gave myself to him, even when I didn't want to. I even sent others to him, knowing full well that he would break them too. All for a shot at my music being heard. Pathetic, isn't it?"

That's when it hit Daniel. He knew who the voice was, and he knew what he had done.

"He called me in the early hours and promised me the biggest gig of my career. It blinded me. It left me wanting more, so I went to meet him. The next thing I knew, I woke up, and I was alone at the side of the road. My belongings were gone, and no matter who I called, nobody would take it further. I was a nobody. Daniel George was a mega star, a celebrity that people like me were told to look up to. That's why little ol' me faded away into the shadows."

Daniel started to sob, but if he could hear it, the person the voice belonged to, the one he had abused and manipulated, ignored it.

"Time passed, and I tried to carry on. I performed my music. I stood on stage with my guitar and played my heart out. Then, one evening, after playing to a minuscule audience of drunks in a silly, run-down pub, there was a letter waiting for me. A cease-and-desist. Apparently, my songs are no longer mine. Daniel George, the voice you've grown up listening to, stole mine and copyrighted them himself, selling them to the highest bidder. Singer after singer appeared at the top of the charts singing my songs, and, no matter what I did or what evidence I showed, nobody would listen."

"Please stop."

"Oh, no, Daniel. We're so close to the end of this story that it would be rude to leave your listeners with a cliffhanger. Do you want to tell them, or shall I?"

There was no reply, only the sound of a desk drawer opening.

"Okay, well, I guess I shall finish the story for your listeners, but I have one small request. Terry, my uncle, was more than willing to help me set this up when I told him what had truly happened. He's the one who locked the door. He's the one who fixed the lines so only I could call in after giving you that one fake call to lure you in. You will find that your drawer is empty and devoid of your normal collection of bottles stolen from the many mini-bars you've stolen from. There is something there that will help you put an end to all of this, but don't use it yet. Allow your listeners the decency that I had taken from me. Allow them to have the ending they want to hear. Let them know there's a happy ending for them, one that I didn't have."

Over the line, there was the sound of the caller yawning before chuckling.

"It was the same old story of me falling to my demons—I drank too much, I took drugs, and I stole to fund my habits. No matter what happened, my life found new and interesting ways to just get lower and to find new ways to punish me. So, with that in mind, we have come to the end of my story, and I can feel my eyes growing heavy from what I've injected in the last few minutes. We have also come to the end of Daniel's story, so if you would be so kind, tell your listeners what you did and say goodbye."

He was sobbing now. The pain of his past had come back to haunt him. A ghost from his past had poured out all his sins for the world to hear, and now he had no choice. There was a thud as the caller dropped their phone, and the line went dead.

Taking a deep breath, he pulled the microphone closer and then pulled the gun from his drawer.

"My name is Daniel George. I have abused, hurt, and paid my way to where I am today, and now my journey is at an end."

In one quick but clumsy movement, he placed the barrel of the gun against his temple and pulled the trigger. His lifeless body slumped in the chair, his brains and fragments of his skull sliding down the wall as the door to the room opened and Terry walked in. The scene in front of him was even worse than he had imagined it would be, but it still brought a smile to his face.

Reaching over and putting on a pair of gloves, he pressed a button, and a song started playing: 'You Can't Always Get What You Want' by The Rolling Stones. The irony wasn't lost on him, but it seemed to put a good emphasis on what he was looking at.

It may not have been the justice that he or his nephew deserved, but at least Daniel George couldn't hurt anyone else again.

Yard Sale Detective

The sun was shining, there were barely any clouds in the sky, and there was a breeze making sure it wasn't too warm.

It was the perfect weather for a yard sale, and that was exactly where Margaret had found herself. She had never been able to resist the allure of a good yard sale.

Her eyes may not have been as sharp as they once were, nor were her hands as quick as they once were, but the thrill of the hunt for something unusual was as strong as ever.

In front of her, on a very full table, was a doll that she just couldn't take her eyes away from. It looked dirty; the paint on its face was chipping, and its clothes looked threadbare. It had dirty-looking curly hair, and its sky blue dress appeared to be more patch than actual dress, so it wasn't particularly special-looking, but there was something in the way it looked at her, with its wonky eyes, that made Margaret fall in love with her instantly.

The doll was clearly an antique, even under the dirt and dust that covered it, but that hadn't even crossed Margaret's mind as she gently picked it up and smiled.

"Hello, my little one, aren't you just precious? What a beauty you are."

Sensing someone else standing in front of her, Margaret looked up and saw the owner of the table watching her like a hawk.

"How much is this wonderful little girl?"

Standing eagerly, her purse ready in her hand to pay, the woman running the yard sale looked shocked that someone would want such a thing, saying that she could have the doll for free.

Before Margaret could say thank you, the woman was gone, as if she had never existed in the first place. So, placing a few coins in a nearby collection tin, one plastered with the logo of a local animal shelter, she gave the doll a hug and began her walk home.

It had been a strange transaction, one that left her feeling a little uneasy, but it was soon forgotten as she kept looking down at the doll, noticing that it seemed to be smiling even more than she remembered it doing before she had picked it up.

As she opened the door to her house, she stopped for a moment to enjoy the warmth of the sun before stepping inside. The walls were lined with framed pictures of dolls, plates with hand painted pictures on them, and even shelves and display cabinets full of every type of doll a person could imagine. Each one was cared for as if they were her own children, each with their own names and clothes.

Margaret gently placed the doll down so that it sat looking at her as she ran a bowl of warm water. She busied herself with getting all the tools she used for cleaning and repairing her dolls and then stood back, looking proudly at the new addition to her collection.

"Let's get you all cleaned up, shall we? I bet we can get you looking just like you used to, if we're careful. Would you like that? Oh, I bet you would, my darling. I bet you would."

Slowly, she took the doll's clothes off, being careful not to rip them as she did. One of the things she liked to do, especially if it was an older doll, was to give them new clothes but keep their tatty old ones sewn up inside them. She'd always thought of it as a way for the doll to keep a part of its old life with it while still finding itself a new, loving home.

With each movement of the tiny cleaning brush, layer upon layer of grime came away from its tiny body, revealing the bright, but scratched, ceramic beneath. Margaret knew that the limbs and features, despite the damage to them, could be easily fixed but had to take care not to break them even more.

After a while, her hands started to ache and throb, but she carried on, determined to make the doll look as beautiful as she would have when she had first been put together.

After drying her off and leaving her to sit next to the sink while she cleaned and put away the tools, Margaret couldn't help but feel her eyes drawn to the damp but now clean doll.

With all the grime now gone, she was able to appreciate the workmanship, the detailing, and the sheer brilliance of how the doll had been made. Even with the chipped paint and the cracks in its body, the doll was absolutely beguiling to her.

Picking the doll up, she felt a sudden warm sensation run through her entire body as she looked down at the doll's bright, startlingly green eyes, leaving her feeling like the doll was alive. Shaking her head and knowing she was just being silly, she walked into the living room and placed the doll on an empty chair. She looked at her for a few moments more, reassuring herself that it really was just a doll, before sitting down herself and pulling out a small box of doll's clothes.

"Oh, yes, we're going to have you looking like a princess in no time."

As she rummaged through the box full of various pieces of clothing, Margaret looked up, sure that she could hear whispering. Sighing, she looked up at the clock, surprised that she'd spent most of the day cleaning the doll.

"Well, I think that's about it for the day for me, darling. I'll find you a nice dress, then I'm going to make myself some dinner and go to bed."

"Okay."

Margaret stared at the doll, unsure if it had just answered her, but she shook her head once more and pulled out a new pale blue dress and, with a delicate hand, dressed her before smiling.

"Perfect. Absolutely perfect."

Pulling a camera out from beside her chair, she took a Polaroid picture of the doll and waited patiently for it to print. As she looked at the picture, Margaret was sure that the doll's smile was even wider, even friendlier, in the photograph itself.

"Just a trick of the light, Margaret. That, or you're just hungry. That's probably it; you're hungry. You're also talking to yourself. That's the first sign of madness."

The quiet, gentle sound of laughter danced around the room before dissipating slowly.

"Yep, definitely hungry. I'm hearing things now."

Leaving the doll on the chair, now wearing its new dress, Margaret made her way into the kitchen and started rattling the pots and pans in preparation for making her dinner.

Cooking was another thing that she enjoyed doing—something that she'd always had a passion for. In fact, her children had always joked that each time they came to visit her, she would have made some new meal, pie, or something else to impress them with.

Coming back with her dinner, she sat down next to the doll and felt happy and content as she switched on the television to watch one of her history shows, this time one about the Romans and how they had lived.

Before she knew it, her eyes jerked open, and Margaret saw that she had fallen asleep. The ticking of the clock seemed loud in the darkness of the evening, but she stood up, stretched, and picked up the doll before making her way to bed.

With the doll in her special place on a shelf facing the bed, Margaret got into bed and felt her eyes grow heavy as she let sleep take her.

Had she kept her eyes open for a few seconds longer, she'd have seen the doll tilt its head and stare at her for a second or two before shutting its own eyes.

***

The sunlight streamed through the bedroom curtains as Margaret stretched and swung her legs out of the bed, putting her slippers on before walking over to the shelf, but the doll wasn't there.

Turning around slowly, she smiled as she saw her sitting on the floor, her eyes looking up at her expectantly.

"Now, how did you get down there, you cheeky madam?"

She picked up the doll, giving it a soft cuddle, and carried her through to the living room, feeling excited at what she had planned for today.

"Well, my cutie, today I'm going to fix the paint on your face and make you even prettier than you already are."

"Thank you."

Again, that quiet voice. It was so low and so gently spoken that it was almost silent.

"You're very welcome," replied Margaret, assuming that she was imagining the voice. That was something she did on occasion; it was really just harmless fun. She knew they couldn't talk, but that didn't mean she had to be rude to them.

Fixing herself a cup of tea, she busied herself by getting out her special paintbrushes—the ones she only used for the most unique of dolls—and her paints. She'd spent years amassing the collection, nearly as long as she had spent creating her groups of dolls, so she took her time choosing just the right brush for the job.

First, she took a sip of tea, something she always did before starting on the painting, and then spent the next few minutes choosing the paint that matched the doll's face best.

"Do you do this for all of us?"

Sighing, slightly annoyed that her mind was wandering and clearly making her hear a non-existent voice, she nodded.

"I do indeed, little one. It's my way of thanking you all for keeping me company."

Margaret pulled out a small pot of paint and grinned excitedly.

"Oh, yes, that's the one. That's just perfect."

Humming to herself—this time it was 'You Sexy Thing' by Hot Chocolate—she took her time painting the doll's face. With each stroke of the brush, the face became brighter, happier, and even content. The green eyes of the doll stared back at her the entire time, making her think that she was being supervised by some big boss.

When she was done, she sat back, grumbling about the ache in her hips, and looked proudly at her work. If she hadn't seen how damaged the face was before, she'd have thought that the doll was nearly new, and that made her happy. It had been in such a state when she'd taken it home that she wasn't even sure it was fixable.

"What do you think?" She asked her as she lifted the doll up to the mirror.

"I'm beautiful."

Margaret gasped. This time, she was sure that the doll's lips had moved when she had spoken.

"I'm sorry, did I scare you? I didn't mean to, I promise. I'm really sorry."

She placed the doll back on the chair gently and backed away from it, unable to take her eyes off it.

"Did you just talk? To me? Did you just..."

Margaret couldn't finish the sentence and, feeling faint from the shock, sat down on the chair opposite.

"I think so. Is that okay?"

She checked her pulse, then drank the rest of her tea before looking at the doll again. She'd tilted her small ceramic head to the side and seemed to be looking at Margaret with an expression almost as confused as hers.

The room was silent for what seemed like forever while they both stared at one another, with Margaret rubbing her eyes.

"How are you talking to me?"

The doll raised its hand to its mouth, as if checking that it was working, before speaking.

"With my mouth."

Despite the weirdness of what was happening, Margaret couldn't help but laugh at the answer the doll had given her. It was so literal and innocent that it felt like a real child was talking. Reaching out, she stroked the doll's face softly, thankful that the paint was dry already.

She could see and hear the doll speaking, but she felt too stunned to do anything other than caress the doll.

"I know this is strange; I'm sorry, but I need to tell you something. It's important, really important; otherwise, I wouldn't have said anything."

The doll's voice had changed somehow. It wasn't low and quiet any more; it was wavering and sad, making Margaret feel worried for the poor little thing in front of her.

"My name's Emily. I used to be a little girl; I think I still am, but I'm a doll too."

All of this sounded like some kind of strange fairytale, one that she would have told her children when they were young.

"What happened?"

Margaret was still not sure if this was really happening, if it made any sense, or—and this was the idea that seemed the most likely—if she was so tired that she was still sleeping and this was just a dream.

"I died. I think. I was ill, and my parents couldn't afford a doctor. They couldn't pay for much. Most of us just did chores for one another or helped each other if we needed to, but nobody could help me."

The way the doll was speaking made Margaret pick it up and give her a gentle yet firm cuddle. She stroked Emily's hair and tried to make reassuring sounds to calm her, as if talking to a small child.

"You poor thing. You poor, poor thing. What happened next? How did you end up in a doll of all things?"

Slowly, Emily turned her head awkwardly and looked at her, her green eyes strangely wet-looking.

"I don't know. I went to sleep and woke up as a doll. I don't like it, but I grew to understand that I, at least, brought some happiness to the children who played with me."

Suddenly, the doll grew stiff in Margaret's hands, and she started to panic.

"Emily, talk to me, sweetheart. I'm here; I promise I'm here; just talk to me."

The doll stayed silent, and she placed her gently on the chair, sitting and waiting for her to speak again, but she didn't.

After a while, Margaret stood up and wiped her eyes with the back of her hand before making herself a cup of tea in an effort to calm her nerves.

The house seemed oddly quiet now that Emily wasn't talking, but she didn't know what to do to make her say anything else. Margaret knew that wasn't all of the story, and she wanted to know what else happened to her as she came back into the room.

"Please, Emily, speak to me. I want to help you."

No words came from the door, so, with a sad look on her face, Margaret placed Emily on her lap and watched the news for a while.

Lunchtime came quickly, as did a visit from Ted, her neighbour. He always seemed to turn up when least expected, but he did always bring cake, so that was a silver lining.

They sat in silence, eating large slices of fruit cake, before he turned and noticed Emily.

"A new one for your collection? You're going to run out of room if you carry on."

He meant nothing by it, but Margaret felt strangely offended by his comment. Her dolls were each equally important to her and kept her company in the house.

"This one's different."

"Aren't they all?" He replied, taking another big bite of cake while looking at Emily. "She's a pretty little thing; I'll give her that much, at least."

"No, I mean it. This one is different. She talks. Her name's Emily."

"Well, that's a bit fancy," replied Ted, seemingly impressed. "How's that work, then? Is it one of those dolls with the string in the back?"

"No, no, she talks. Really talks. She's alive."

Ted raised one of his bushy eyebrows, a sign that he wasn't sure if Margaret was making a joke at his expense or not.

"I'm sure she is."

Growing impatient and frustrated with the fact that Ted was clearly not believing her, she looked at Emily sadly and dropped the subject. They had an hour or so of small talk before he made his way out, but he stopped at the front door.

"Are you okay? Like, really okay?"

She nodded and tried to usher him out of the house as politely as possible, feeling guilty at the relief he had finally left.

"Emily, darling. It's okay. It's just me. Talk to me, my lovely, talk to me," she said as she rushed back into the room.

On the chair, Emily had flopped lifelessly onto her side, but as Margaret spoke, the doll's body stiffened and jerked. She reached out to touch her, but there was a strange sense of energy coming from the doll itself, and Emily sat upright, her ceramic face looking terrified.

"I remember, I remember it."

Margaret picked her up and held her close to her chest to try to comfort her.

"Remember what?"

"They couldn't pay for my medicine, so, in exchange for a stranger paying, my parents let him take me to the circus he owned and put me to work there."

There was no way for her to believe what she was hearing. It was heartbreaking. How could someone do that to their own child?

"I performed tricks, I danced, and the magic man let me be the person that was sawn in half. It was fun at first, but they worked me until I couldn't work any more. I hurt everywhere; I couldn't sleep; then I woke up as a doll."

Margaret could feel herself crying, and her tears dripped down onto Emily's head.

"I am so sorry. That's horrible, just horrible."

For the next few minutes, they both stayed silent and just held each other. The more she spoke, the worse Emily's story sounded.

"I've watched people come and go," she said again, this time her voice quieter, "and I tried to be the best doll I could be, but I want to go home now."

The way she said home and the way her voice cracked told Margaret everything she needed to know. She knew that she had to help this poor soul, had to help her find some way back to her family, or at the very least, let her rest in peace.

"How can I help you? Please, let me help."

Again, Emily's body turned stiff, and she became silent and cold, leaving Margaret to hold the doll close to her chest and become lost in her thoughts.

***

The night came and went without Emily speaking any more. Margaret had placed her on the same shelf as before and tried to sleep, but all she could manage was a couple of hours of fitful sleep at most.

When the dreams did come, they weren't good ones. Instead, Margaret dreamed of poor Emily being left at the circus, where she would perform on the stage until she was too tired to do any more. She dreamed of lying cold and alone until she closed her eyes for the final time. At times, it felt like she was there with her, watching everything unfold in front of her eyes. It felt so real that she could have reached out and touched the things in front of her.

Waking in the morning, she felt exhausted, but with a sense of determination running through her thoughts. She wanted to find out as much as she could about the circus—about where it had been and where it had gone—so she could find out what happened to Emily. It was almost like a compulsion to find out and help her.

For most of the morning, the doll was silent and didn't move, no matter how much Margaret spoke to her.

The atmosphere in the house felt heavy and oppressive as she paced around, trying to figure out what to do next.

No matter how many cups of tea she drank or how many times she walked around the house, it just didn't make sense. It felt so final and so heartbreaking that it was almost helpless.

Sitting down in front of the computer that her daughter had bought her the year before, Margaret did the one thing she could think of. She tried to search for some sort of history about the circuses that had come through town, but it was useless. There were so many that she was just going around in circles.

Grabbing her jacket, she made her way back to the yard where she had bought Emily, but when she knocked on the door, the owner of the house knew nothing of the woman or even the yard sale that had happened on her lawn.

Sitting on a nearby bench, Margaret started to doubt herself.

Had the doll really spoken to her?

Had she even bought the doll here, or had she already owned it?

None of this made even the tiniest amount of sense to her, especially with nobody knowing anything about the yard sale. She couldn't even remember the charity box that she'd put her donation into. It was just another dead end.

Seeing her sitting forlornly outside, a young man came out of the church across the road and, with a friendly smile on his face, asked if she was okay.

The kindness the stranger showed her made Margaret burst into tears and explain everything that had happened in between the deep and sad sobs that racked her entire body.

"Have you thought about looking at missing person reports?"

It was such a simple suggestion from the man, but one that took her by surprise. The one problem was that she only had the name Emily to go by. That and the fact that she had apparently performed at an unnamed circus.

"We have a computer in the church; I can help you look if you want."

When Margaret looked up, she saw the young man holding out his hand to her. The brightness of the dog collar around his neck and the nearly flawless condition of his shirt told her that he was new to the church but had taken great pride in his appearance.

"You believe me?"

The man just smiled before replying. "Why wouldn't I? I have no reason not to; besides, belief has nothing to do with kindness. You're upset, and if helping you out with a few computer searches here and there helps, then I am more than happy to do that."

Margaret watched with amazement as the man typed faster than she had ever seen before. The way his fingers hovered over the keys was like an intricate dance being performed in front of her eyes.

Within moments, he had a pile of printouts on the table and had started to read through them.

"Right, your doll sounds very much like it would be from the turn of the century," he said, pointing to a photo of a doll that looked like Emily; only this one was in a museum in the next town over. "That, at least, narrows down our searches a little."

Taking a couple of sheets of paper herself, Margaret began to read about the travelling groups and shows that had come through in that time period, only stopping when one felt like they didn't match the criteria she was looking for.

After a few minutes, she gasped, and a tear rolled down her cheek. On the paper in her hand was a grainy, old-looking photograph of some performers on a tiny, wooden stage. One of them was a small girl, no older than ten or eleven at the most, who somehow managed to look like Emily, the doll.

Standing up so quickly that it startled the young man, Margaret threw her arms around him and rushed out of the church before coming back in with a sheepish look on her face.

"Sorry, I forgot to say thank you. That was very rude of me. I appreciate this so much, and I'm sure Emily will as well."

Nodding his head slowly, the man looked at her with a kind smile. "I hope so too."

Margaret made her way back to the house as quickly as she could manage, ignoring the aches and pains. She would deal with those later, but this was much more important.

"Emily, Emily, my love. I think I found something that can help you."

Stepping into the bedroom, she saw that the doll had slumped forward, its tiny ceramic head in its hands.

"It's okay, I promise. It will all be okay."

She picked Emily up gently and waited for her to open her eyes. When she did, Margaret smiled at her.

"Are you ready to go home? I've had an idea. I really think it's a good one. Look."

She excitedly pulled the folded-up piece of paper out of her pocket and showed Emily.

"That's you, isn't it? If we find where this picture was taken, then maybe we'll find out how to help you."

Margaret heard the doorbell and sighed. It would be Ted again with those cakes, appearing in the hope of a cup of tea and a session of complaining about how the world was turning into something awful. It was always the same thing. Food cost too much, television shows and movies weren't as good as they used to be, and the music of today was just noise. She wondered which one it would be this time.

As Ted walked in, he made himself at home by serving out the cake and switching the kettle on.

Margaret ignored him while she read through more of the papers, but when he came in, Ted stopped mid-step and pointed at the piece of paper in her hand.

"I've not seen that place for years. My dad used to take me there each time the circus came through town."

She looked up in shock, then over at Emily, unsure of what to say.

"Oh, the shows they used to have there. Dancers, jugglers, clowns, and even fellas that could spit fire high into the air. What a show! You don't get anything like that these days, do you?"

Emily nodded silently at Margaret, being careful not to let Ted see her move.

"Is it nearby? I'd love to take a stroll down there some time. I bet it would look beautiful in the weather we're having right now."

If Margaret was trying to sound subtle, then it really wasn't working, as Ted looked over at her with a wry smile on his face.

"Say, what are you up to? You look like one of those detectives on TV when they get a lead."

"Oh, nothing. Just going a bit stir crazy in the house, is all."

Trying to change the subject, Margaret took a great big bite of the cake, a very moist Battenberg that Ted had made himself, and made happy little noises as she chewed.

"This is divine, Ted. Your best one yet."

That seemed to do it, as the man beamed the cheesiest smile that she had ever seen him do. He was a simple man with simple pleasures in life, and baking was one of them. If you wanted to get him to change the subject, just tell him that the cake he'd made was nice. It had worked on him for years, and she wasn't going to change now.

"Fancy some company on your stroll, or are you taking your little friend over there?"

Before Margaret could reply, Emily had stood up, pointed right at Ted with a tiny ceramic hand, and cleared her throat.

"I'm a big girl; thank you very much. I will go with her."

Instead of being shocked or maybe even scared by the doll's movement, Ted just clapped his hands gleefully, whooping and hollering like a big kid.

"Oh, how splendid, how wonderful! My word. How did you do that? That was brilliant. No wonder you have so many dolls if you can do tricks like that with them."

With a nod, Emily flopped back down on the chair and, much to her clear annoyance, pretended to be just like any other doll in Margaret's collection.

"Erm, well, practice, I suppose. It's a new, and rather unexpected, hobby of mine."

Finishing off his chunk of cake and taking one last look at Emily, Ted stood up and chuckled to himself.

"Well, it's just a flying visit today, my dear. I got to get to the doctors; perhaps they'll even see me on time for once. You never know; miracles have happened, right?"

As he made his way to leave, Ted stopped and smiled at Margaret. "You'll just have to simply tell me how you did that. What a wonderful trick!"

Walking up the path, she watched until he was out of sight, still chuckling at Emily's outburst, before shutting the front door and taking a deep breath.

That was a close one. He would never believe that the doll had actually spoken; he hadn't believed her when she tried to tell him before.

Emily tapped her on the leg, but her tiny face looked worried. Margaret looked down at her, matching the expression with one of her own.

This was happening too fast; what if it was the wrong place?

What if this was the one chance she had to release Emily?

Leaning down to pick her up, Margaret could feel every single ache and pain that the last few days had revealed to her. Her entire body felt heavy and tired, but with one look at that tiny painted face with its bright green eyes, she knew that she would do all she could to help the child trapped in the doll.

"Fancy a walk?"

***

It took them a bus ride and then a thirty-minute walk, but, with the help of directions from people confused by why they wanted to go there, Margaret and Emily found themselves standing in an empty field.

Even now, the ground looked misshapen and bumpy from the number of wheels, steps, and more that had made their way through over the years, carving their history into the very mud itself.

Despite the sun beating down on them both, Margaret felt herself shiver as a sense of fear ran through her. Emily, held tightly in her arms, felt icy cold to the touch.

It was just a field. That's all it was. A well-used, now deserted field. That's all. It was empty, overgrown in places, and mostly forgotten, yet it brought with it a sense of dread, heavy enough to threaten them both by pushing them into the ground to be forgotten.

The strange thing was, it felt like Margaret had been here before—many times in fact—but she never had been. There was a nervous energy coming from Emily, one that had started to make her vibrate, but she didn't say a word. Instead, she just looked around with her glassy green eyes as wide as they possibly could be.

"I'm scared. I don't want to be here."

Margaret stroked her hair gently, the coldness of the doll shocking her, but she tried her best smile to reassure her. She could say that everything was going to be okay and that she would keep her safe, but she wasn't even sure if she believed it herself. She wasn't even sure she knew what she was doing, but somehow it felt right to be here.

"Does any of this look familiar to you? Do you know where we need to look?"

Emily's mouth opened to say something in reply, but her body went stiff once more, her eyes looking up into the bright sky above them.

The clouds seemed to slow as they drifted across the sky, the sun grew brighter, and Margaret found herself staring at the doll. She held her protectively and looked around the field, trying to find a sign of what to do. To her, it was just a normal field. It had been used again and again. It had held show after show and event after event. Now, it has been forgotten and left behind, much like the memories it once helped create.

"Tree."

The voice was quiet, strained, and breathless, as if the word required a monumental amount of effort to say.

"Tree."

Again, that word, but this time it sent a shiver down Margaret's spine.

"I've got you, sweetheart. We'll find it. Don't you worry."

She didn't know what made her do it; she didn't know why she chose that particular direction, but she started walking further into the disused field. Brambles scratched at her legs, and branches from the overgrown bushes picked at their clothes as they walked past, but it didn't stop her. Margaret knew she had to find the tree; there was a compulsion running through her, giving her a sense of determination that she hadn't felt in years.

"We'll find it. Don't worry. I promise we'll find it, darling."

A few steps in front of them, a tree beckoned ominously. Margaret was sure that it hadn't been there before; it wasn't something that a person could easily miss, but there was something dark and disturbing about how it seemed to want to pull them both towards it.

In her arms, Emily started to jerk and vibrate, with sadness coming from her tiny body. The closer they got to the tree, the more the doll moved.

Margaret looked the tree up and down and knew what she had to do. Kneeling, with a groan of pain as her joints clicked with the effort, she sat Emily at the foot of the tree, amongst the roots. Instantly, the doll began to glow, and she tried to stand on her own two feet before opening her mouth to speak.

"Here. I'm here."

Instantly, the doll fell to the floor with a thud, and Margaret rushed forward to pick her up. The ceramic body was icy cold, and the doll felt heavier than it ever had before. The ground seemed to open and move of its own accord, the mud undulating in front of them. It churned and hissed as a flash of dull white revealed itself.

Snatching her phone from her pocket, she made the call she knew would bring a whole load of questions that she wouldn't be able to answer, but with it, she hoped that it would bring the chance for Emily to rest peacefully.

***

Days passed, and Margaret found herself the subject of many interviews, each one making her feel more awkward than the last.

She'd told them all that she was a rambler and had stumbled on the dirt after being disturbed, but the one thing she couldn't explain was the absence of the tree. It wasn't there when they came to exhume the little bones from the ground.

There was a lot of media interest in the remains having been found; they framed it as a story of a child's lost hope for happiness and safety, and it soon became one of the highest-rated reports they'd held on the news channels that showed it.

They were so desperate for more information and for ways to fill the airtime that they interviewed anybody they could get to talk to, including Ted. He, of course, loved the attention and even described himself as a baker and historical expert, despite never having taken any interest in the latter at all before now.

After a while, the dust settled and the news went on to newer stories that would pique the viewers interest, but Margaret never forgot that day. Instead, she was there when they gave Emily a proper burial. She shed a tear for the loss but felt a sense of happiness that the poor soul had finally found peace.

Once she knew they were alone in the cemetery, she brought out the plaque that she had bought herself. They hadn't been able to find Emily's name and had given her a nameless gravestone with a Bible quote on it. The stone looked so lifeless that it made her heart ache.

Opening the plastic bag she had brought with her, Margaret brought out a small, hand-carved cross with a plaque on it that read, "Emily, a beloved and kind soul. Gone but never forgotten" on it and pushed it into the ground in front of the gravestone.

"There you go, my darling. It's not much, I'm afraid, but I hope you like it."

She spent a couple of hours sitting next to the grave, telling Emily all about her day, including news of the new cake that Ted had made, and drinking tea from a small tartan flask she'd brought with her.

When it began to grow darker, Margaret said her goodbyes and made her way home. From that night on, Margaret could feel a warmth radiating from the doll. She knew that Emily had finally found peace, but she missed her terribly.

She kept the doll on a shelf in her living room, where it seemed to glow with a new vitality, its eyes a brighter green than she had ever seen before. And every now and then, when the night was quiet, Margaret would hear the faint sound of a child's laughter coming from the doll, and it made her smile, safe in the knowledge that Emily was happy now.

Like and Subscribe

With his eyes wide with excitement, John looked at the building in front of him.

The windows were boarded up clumsily, there was a metal chain-link fence around the entire place, multiple locks on the door, and it looked like a stiff would blow it all down at any minute.

It was perfect.

Pulling a small, hand-held camera from his backpack, he turned it on to film himself and put on his best smile for the people who would watch later that night when he uploaded it to his YouTube channel.

"Hello, you sexy beasts. We have found the perfect place to explore. It looks like something out of a 1950s horror movie. In fact, I'm half expecting Vincent Price or someone like that to greet us when we get our asses over that fence. Well, here goes."

Switching the camera off, he looked over his shoulder at his companion, a big, awkward lump of a man named Russ. He was a man with a permanently serious look on his bearded face. He wasn't even sure if he'd ever seen the man smile in the entire time they had worked together. It was even a running joke on the channel.

They'd heard about this place thanks to one of the comments on their last video and travelled out to the city limits to check it out. There was an outlandish story about it being haunted too, one that seemed too good to be true, but it was a great opportunity to make some more spooky content for the channel. That always seemed to go over well with the viewers, even if they did have to fake some of the noises and paranormal moments themselves.

Russ cleared his throat and nodded towards the fence. He was a man of few words, but John knew exactly what he meant. It was time to try to climb over them. The small mercy was that, this time, these fences didn't have rusty barbed wire on them like in the last video. That had cost him his favourite pair of jeans, even leading to a video where he lamented their loss. Strangely, it had garnered one of the highest view counts they'd had in weeks.

John handed Russ the camera, instructing him not to turn it on until he was halfway up the fence, earning a roll of Russ' eyes as a reply.

Climbing up the fence and wondering why there wasn't an easier way into the decrepit old building, John wondered if he should have paid more attention in the fitness classes he paid for—the very same ones where he half-assed every exercise they gave him.

Seeing him struggling to get a leg over the top of the fence, Russ turned the camera on and, with a wry smile, told him that they were rolling.

John swore under his breath and then balanced precariously atop the fence and began his spiel, in the hopes it would entice people to watch when they uploaded the video.

"Here we are, mere steps from the hospital. Russ is filming, and I'm finding us a better way in. Together, we are going to find out what haunts this grand place of healing. What lost souls are wandering around inside? What heartbreaking stories will we find? Well, my fellow 'Spirit Wranglers,' let's see what we can find."

John had always hated the name for the channel and the viewers, but they used it as a joke, and it stuck, soon becoming their brand to such an extent that even their truck had it emblazoned on the sides.

Swinging himself over the fence and dropping down a lot more gracefully than he had climbed up, he looked at Russ, who was already busy putting the camera in the backpack in preparation for his climb.

The larger man took a run up, grabbed hold of the fence links, and was over it in mere seconds, feeling impressed with himself, much to John's annoyance.

"Show off," he said sarcastically as Russ pulled the camera back out and switched it on. He took a deep breath and carried on the showman routine that he had long since perfected for the channel and its fans. "Now that Russ has finally gotten over the fence," he said with a bitchy tone, "let's see if we can get inside."

The look on Russ' face told him everything he needed to know about how annoyed his business partner was, but John knew that he would soon forget the insult once he'd been given his money.

As they both stood in front of the doors, they couldn't help but feel a sense of sadness that such a place had obviously been forgotten and left to rot. The doors looked like they would have been stunning to see in all their glory, but here, they looked like a quick kick would make them crumble like wet cardboard.

Russ looked over his shoulder, sure that he had sensed someone behind him, but he shook his head when he saw that there wasn't anyone there. Despite his size and gruff demeanour, he'd always been one to be quite jumpy and easily spooked, not that he'd ever admit it to anyone.

John rolled his eyes and snapped his fingers to get Russ' attention, then waited for the camera to be pointing at him once more.

"Could you imagine what this place must have looked like in its heyday? It must have looked like a beacon of hope for all the sick, injured, and dying. Hell, maybe to some, it must have looked like heaven on earth in their time of need."

He jiggled the locks slightly, the noise telling him that it wouldn't take much for them to break off, and he knew that he could put on a show.

"Russ, my dear, let's get this open and check inside. I wonder if the inside is in as much disrepair as the outside."

Feeling the weight of the crowbar in his hand, he held it up theatrically above his head before bringing it down on the padlocks, which broke off instantly.

Russ zoomed in on the remains of the locks before reaching forward and pushing the doors open. The squeak of the hinges felt obscenely loud, and he flinched as John played up to the camera, pretending to look concerned as he poked his head inside the dark building.

"As you can see, it's rather dark in here, so we'll have to be careful, but, as you regular viewers know, the darkness brings us more chances to communicate with the dearly departed."

Russ hated how annoyingly over the top John was when he presented the videos. He was more of a person who spoke when she needed to, but John seemed incapable of remaining silent and allowing the moment to unfold.

As the light on the camera flicked on, the hallway burst into a dim glow, revealing torn paper on the floor and peeling paint on the walls, accompanied by the scurrying sound of the rats and others who lived in the darkness.

The further they came into the hospital, with Russ closing the door, more debris came into view. rusty equipment, broken chairs, even smashed mirrors. It was as if the people here had left in a hurry, leaving everything behind.

"Is anything in this place not broken? Maybe it's what gives this place such a creepy vibe."

John's words hung in the air for a moment before giving way to a sense of uneasiness, almost as if something were watching their every move.

The footsteps came first. Their low, foreboding echo seemed to resonate around them both before they heard the scraping sound of something being dragged across the floor, something heavy, but they could only see their own shadows.

Russ showed the camera around the hallway, its light illuminating the dust in the air and showing them just how dirty and forgotten the place was. It also showed them that they were alone. John walked slightly ahead, pretending to read some of the dirty pieces of paper hanging at strange angles, but he jumped back.

"Russ, look at this man; it's fucked up."

Walking slowly towards him, Russ sighed and pointed the camera at John and then at the wall, making sure everything was in frame perfectly.

"Great, now we're going to have to beep you out and then censor this," he said, pointing at the words on the wall.

They had been crudely spray painted on there, and time had dulled the redness of the paint, but the words were clear to see, and John felt a mixture of fear and excitement.

FUCKING MURDERING BASTARDS!

"Russ, dude, that ties in with the comment from GhostLover82. They said there had been deaths here from as far back as the 1950s."

"I'm sure all our viewers know that we won't jump to conclusions. We investigate, then we show our findings."

John sighed and touched the painted letters. They felt strangely warm to his finger tips, making his entire hand tingle.

"Dude, it feels hot."

Turning the camera away, the light cut through the corridor, and Russ tried to focus on something else, letting the beam pick out some of the rusted, bent pieces of equipment.

John followed him, touching everything he walked past, feeling confused as his body alternated between feeling hot and cold.

The sound of scraping grew louder, and both Russ and John looked around, trying to focus the camera on where they thought the noise was coming from.

Following its echo, they came to a door. Somehow it managed to look askew yet close tightly at the same time. Russ tried the handle, and it opened slowly.

Stepping into the room, it looked like an office, with bits of paper and open files everywhere. There were footsteps in the dust, leaving prints on the files and the paperwork.

"As you can see," John said, trying to sound like a serious reporter or even a presenter on a highbrow documentary, "it looks like someone has been here before us. I wonder if they found anything."

Looking up at the sound of the camera being switched off, John noticed Russ holding it down by his side. Without the light showing that they were filming, the room felt oppressive and much smaller than it actually was.

"I don't like this, John. We should get out of here. We'll make something up. It's not like they'll be able to tell the difference; most of the people who watch our shit don't even believe us any way."

With the way he had said that and the way Russ was looking at him, John felt defeated and empty. This was their life; this had been the one thing they had always wanted to do together, and now, just because of a tiny set of footprints in the mess left behind, Russ wanted to quit.

"Look, we'll give it ten more minutes, add some random as fuck effects to the video, then call it a night. Hell, let's go get a drink after this, yeah?"

Russ sighed and brought the camera back up to face John, but he didn't look happy about it.

"Fine, but ten minutes, and that's it."

The light clicked back on, and he smiled for the camera as Russ held it steady.

"There's a strange atmosphere here. It's heavy and, dare I say, sad as it clings to us in this office."

The scraping sound intensified, and they both turned around in shock as the echo danced past the open office door. It was moving around the building; they were sure of it, and this time, it wasn't one of their tricks.

Slowly, with Russ so close that he nearly walked into his back, John made his way out of the office, only stopping to take a look at some more words sprayed on a different wall.

THEY WILL TAKE YOU NEXT!

YOU WILL SUFFER!

These words were brighter but more jagged, clearly having been sprayed in a hurry.

"As you can see, someone is having fun at other urban explorers' expense, but that will not stop us. We will find out if the stories of unkempt spirits with souls too heavy to leave are true."

Turning to face the camera and leaning forward until his nose was nearly touching the camera, John grinned.

"This, my friends, looks like it's going to be one of the scariest, most spine-tingling adventures we've been on since we started the channel. I hope you will stay with us for the whole video."

As they walked down the corridor, with Russ trying to film everything he could in the hopes he would catch something on camera, the sound grew louder and louder.

In front of them was a large door, but it looked different from the others. It was intact, it was locked, and it looked well maintained. Both Russ and John looked at one another, neither wanting to touch the door handle.

The sound appeared to be coming from the room, yet they stood there silently for a few moments.

With a deep sigh, Russ handed the camera over and then tried to open the door. The handle burned his skin as soon as he touched it, and he swore. On the palm of his hand was a dark, brown scar.

Leaning forward, John zoomed in on the scar and took a deep breath. This was going even better than he had hoped, leaving him sure that they were going to be inundated with new subscribers to the channel.

"As you can see, something strange is happening here, and you know what happens when we find something strange? We find answers!"

The earlier hesitation, the earlier fear, had dissipated, only to be replaced with a deep-seated compulsion to open that door and march inside.

Russ took a step back as the door opened without either of them touching it, choosing to grab the camera instead and focus in on the door again, the light struggling to cut through the shadows in the room.

Even squinting, they could barely make out anything other than some jagged shapes, leaving their minds to wander. Each step they took echoed and mixed with the scraping sound that they were trying to follow.

"I don't like this, John. Something's wrong."

"It's what the viewers want, Russ. They want the dangerous; they want the strange and unexplained. Suck it up and follow me. I know what I'm doing."

Checking his watch, Russ saw it had been much longer than the ten minutes they had agreed on, but he knew when John had an idea in his head, there was no shifting him.

"Fine, but we're doing this room, and that's it. We're done. Channel or not, I'm not putting us in danger just to get a few extra viewer comments."

Ignoring the nay saying, John walked further into the darkness, swearing loudly when he tripped over a rusty I.V. pole. Struggling to get back to his feet, he saw a thick file on the floor. It seemed out of place, like something too convenient to find, but the excitement took over his thoughts, and he opened it.

The papers in the file were dated from the 1950s, yet the paper looked newly printed. It couldn't have looked more out of place unless it had a big neon sign saying "put here on purpose" above it.

Each page had a photograph stapled to it and smudged typing under it. The pages had clearly been written using an old-fashioned typewriter and related the stories of the patients in the pictures.

The photographs were all different; some clearly showed people who had been treated here, while others showed people who worked in the hospital, but each page was detailed to the point where you knew almost everything about a person.

"Well, that's strange. This looks new, but everything else looks old, mangled, and falling apart. It doesn't make sense."

"Maybe it's someone just playing a prank?"

Russ had made a good point. It could be someone from another channel doing it to steal some of their viewers or subscribers. It wouldn't have been the first time. The community was strangely competitive, even cut-throat at times.

"Good point; we can't help it if someone is feeling a bit jealous, can we, folks?"

They spent the next couple of minutes rummaging around the messy, dusty room, but there was nothing else worth noting for their video. It was just a collection of broken furniture, pictures hanging at strange angles on the walls, and even pens and empty notepads scattered around.

"Who works here? An author?" Russ asked sarcastically, making John laugh hysterically. If it had been anyone else asking, it wouldn't have been anywhere near as funny.

Gesturing towards the door, they found their way back into the corridor, but something seemed different. Around them, the atmosphere felt violent in a way that caused their bodies to feel rooted to the spot.

John couldn't explain the sudden change, nor could Russ, who was still busy trying to catch as much of it as he could on the camera. The air around them smelled rancid, and a sudden chill came over them both.

It was Russ who pointed first. A previously shut door was wide open, and a light had been switched on. It bathed what they could see of the room's interior in a dirty-looking grey light. Before he could say anything, he watched as John rushed towards the room like an overexcited child.

He ran to catch up with his friend, but the door slammed shut just before he could get to it, leaving him to impact against it and fall to the floor, sending the camera flying out of his hands and skidding across the floor.

"Very fucking funny, Russ. Real fucking hilarious. Now open the door and get to filming this shit show. This room is insane, man. It's like something out of a damned horror movie. Where's Boris Karloff when we need him, huh?"

"I didn't close it. Why the fuck would I, you idiot? I told you we should get out of here, but did you listen? No," he replied as he scrambled about in the darkness, trying to find the camera. "If my shits broken because of that, you're paying for it."

Relief washed over him when his hand touched the camera strap, and he pulled it closer to himself, swearing when he saw that the lens was cracked.

"You've fucked the lens, man. That's going to cost you. Now, open the damned door. This isn't funny."

"I didn't shut it, you idiot. There's some cool shit in here that would look amazing on our channel. It's fucked up to hell in here."

Once more, Russ tried the handle, but it wouldn't budge, not even an inch. Something was very wrong.

"I'm going to find another way around, John. I'll get you, then we're getting out of here."

"Film everything, Russ, and I mean everything."

He walked off, shaking his head, not believing that John was ignoring the signs telling them to chalk this visit up as a mistake. He wasn't exactly known for admitting his mistakes, either.

Waiting for the sound of Russ' footsteps to fade away, John went back to rummaging through the room.

In the middle of it was a large, reclining exam chair. Attached to the arms were cracked leather restraints with troubling, dark stains on them. The chair itself looked ancient, like something that should have been in a museum. There was also a strange smell coming from it—a mixture of stale urine and the clinical aroma of the cleaning supplies these places always seemed to use.

It was the files and the handwritten notes that he was most interested in. They told horrific stories of experimental treatments and of people being used to operate on in an effort to find cures for the most dangerous of maladies.

He pulled his phone out of his pocket and put it in selfie mode, smiling as it recorded.

"Guys, I've somehow gotten separated from Russ, so while he's off on his own adventure, I'll be filming on my phone. On the plus side, how cool is this room? He said this excitedly as he filmed the room, pointing out the straps on the chair, describing the smells, and really putting on a show for the imaginary audience. "Something tells me that maybe, just maybe, this place wasn't all about healing."

Lowering the phone slightly and using his best attempt at a respectful voice, he described the rest of the room.

"There's a strange smell in here too, like some kind of Hell-sent dentist's surgery."

Walking towards the back of the room, trying his best to ignore how cold it had become in the last couple of moments, John noticed another door but wasn't surprised to find it locked.

"Well, surprise, surprise, another locked door. I don't know about you lot, but this is getting boring now," he said into the phone, making sure to film himself trying the door handle again.

A scratching sound behind the door made John jump back, nearly dropping the phone in the process. For a moment, he stood silently and tried to calm his breathing. Swallowing deeply, he lifted the phone back up to his face and smiled, trying his best to play it off as an overreaction.

"Sorry about that. I think this place is getting to me and fraying my nerves a bit. It happens to the best of us."

The scratching grew louder and more insistent before stopping as suddenly as it had started. In the blink of an eye, all the lights in the room turned on, taking John by surprise, and he swore loudly when he saw a giant cross with a crucified version of Jesus hanging from it. Making sure to catch a glimpse of it with the camera, he wondered how he managed to miss such a large thing on the wall.

"Looks like someone was rather religious in here, which is not surprising considering it was a hospital, I suppose."

Reaching out a hand, John touched it and was surprised that it didn't feel as cold as the rest of the room. As soon as his fingers touched it, the surface seemed to give slightly.

"Now, I've seen enough horror movies to know that a huge fucking Jesus isn't always a good thing, so," John turned his back to the carving as he spoke, "I'm going to have another look around to see if I can get out of here."

He hoped he was doing enough to hide the wavering fear in his voice, but, and this was a small silver lining, it made the video all the more authentic if they knew he was spooked.

There had to be a key somewhere in the room; there just had to be one. If not, then he was going to kick the damned door down himself, or at least try to.

"I know the way out of here. You just have to trust me."

John stopped immediately as soon as he heard the voice. It was low and quiet, with a slight accent that wouldn't have been out of place in an old British movie from the 1950s.

"Who's there? If this is a prank, then be aware that I am filming and it will be going up on my channel."

"I know the way out of here. You just have to trust me," the voice repeated. This time it sounded more insistent, almost disappointed that he hadn't immediately done as he was told.

John didn't want to move. It seemed all too convenient that someone was making noises outside and that he could now hear a voice, and the doors to this room were locked. It was a prank. It had to be. Ghosts don't really exist. He knew that. Hell, he'd made a small fortune making videos about breaking into abandoned buildings and playing up to the cameras about how spooky they were.

"I know the way out of here. You just have to trust me."

"Look, the fun's over; I'm bored now. As cool as the old medical equipment is, I've got better things to do with my time," he replied, making sure that the camera on his phone was focused solely on his face. He wasn't exactly a good actor, but that didn't mean that he couldn't make himself look good.

"Then you trust me. Good. I will release you."

"Oh, how very fucking kind of you! John snapped sarcastically.

The door didn't open like he had expected it to, and he sighed loudly.

"That was rude. If there's one thing I don't like, young man, it's rudeness. I will take you downstairs myself."

The loud sound of wood cracking behind him made John spin around, dropping the phone on the floor as the lights flickered erratically.

All he could do was watch as the carving started to shake, its paint flaking off in large clumps to reveal mottled flesh. In one movement, it yanked its feet from the crucifix, the nails staying embedded in his skin, and jumped down to the floor.

With each step towards John that it took, the thing dragged the crucifix behind him. The nails in his feet dragged against the floor, leaving deep scratches. His hands were still nailed to the wood, but it didn't seem to slow him down at all.

"No, no, no. This is bullshit. This isn't happening. You're just some sort of special effect or something."

The man smiled as he came closer, his footsteps taking on a wet, squelching sound as he walked. Looking John in the eyes, he pulled a hand away from the wood and reached out to him.

There was nowhere to run; both doors were still locked as he pounded on them and demanded to be let out.

A cold, wet hand grabbed his shoulder and turned him around violently, leaning his face as close to John as possible, making the YouTuber gag as the smell of rotten flesh assaulted him.

Raising a hand to his mouth, the dead man in front of him bit the top of the nail in his hand and pulled it slowly from his flesh. Yanking his other hand from the wood, he left the crucifix to drop loudly to the floor.

John didn't move; he didn't say anything; he just stared at the creature in front of him. There was no fight left in him, so when he grabbed him by the shoulders, he let him do it.

Clumsily, he was laid down on the crucifix, and he felt his thoughts twist and become little more than a jumbled mess. His movements were no longer his own.

In two swift moves, the man forced the nails through his hands and into the wood as John screamed out in pain, drowning out the low battery warning from the phone on the floor.

The last thing he saw was the man lifting up the cross to hang it back where it had been. Then his world turned black.

***

Russ had walked up and down the corridor multiple times, trying each door that he passed. Each time he repeated his steps, he hoped that, beyond all reason, one of the doors would open, but it never did.

"Russ, Russ, come down here. I've found something really fucking cool."

It was John's voice, but there seemed to be something different about it. Its tone was strained, almost like it was feigning excitement for some reason.

In front of him, the corridor grew brighter, and the door at the end opened slowly to reveal some stairs. On the walls, in brightly painted letters, was a warning.

EVERYTHING IS A LIE.

WALK DOWN THESE STAIRS TO MEET YOUR END.

REMEMBER TO CLOSE YOUR EYES.

FOR YOUR TIME HAS COME.

AND ALL MUST DIE.

"Come downstairs. It's brilliant down here. It's going to look so good on film."

Walking down the steps, Russ couldn't shake the feeling that someone—or something—was following him down there. The voice at the back of his mind was telling him to turn and run away; every fibre of his being was screaming at him that this wasn't safe, but he knew that he couldn't leave John down there. As annoyingly arrogant as he was, he was one of his best friends.

Finding himself in the basement of the building, Russ felt like he had ended up in a horror cliché, but stopped when a freezing cold gust of wind forced itself through his body.

That's when he saw it—a dim but flickering light in the corner of the room. He took a step forward but stopped when he heard high-pitched laughter.

It was a strange feeling to know that you weren't alone, yet your brain was still telling you that there was nobody there. It made his heart beat loudly in his chest, feeling like it was going to make its way up his throat until he vomited it out onto the cold, dirty floor.

"Come closer, and I will take you to your friend. I promise. He's safe."

There was something in the way the voice spoke to him that made him feel afraid. It was soft, but there was no kindness in its words.

"C'mon Russ. Don't leave me here alone; you're missing out. I thought we were friends."

With each word that John said and the way they echoed around the room, the light in the corner flickered quicker and became brighter.

A woman stepped out of the darkness and gracefully walked towards him, her hands held out in greeting. Her face was pale, her eyes bright yet lifeless. She had scars all over her face and arms.

Against his better judgement, Russ walked towards her, feeling entranced by her spectral appearance but also curious if what he was seeing was really there.

"This place, oh, you should have seen it. It was a thing of beauty. People flocked to us in the hopes that we could use our knowledge to cure their ills and maybe even make them into better people."

She looked at Russ and reached out, taking his face in her hands.

"Look. Watch. Learn."

His eye rolled back into his head, and Russ' entire body shook from the effort that the visions were putting him through.

With each blink, he saw something new — something grotesque and brutal. He felt sick to his stomach as he saw people getting operated on while awake, their screams echoing in his ears.

There were scenes of blood and lumps of flesh being dumped into black garbage bags and thrown into bins as they sliced and cut into their patients. No matter how much he wanted to, he couldn't look away.

All around him, the basement had turned into a tired-looking, blood-covered surgical area. He stood by the door, looking at the woman who had been in front of Russ only moments ago, but her scars were gone. She wore an apron over her uniform, and her hands were inside some blood-soaked rubber gloves.

The whole scene was complete chaos. There was a body, its stomach open and revealing its guts under the harsh overhead light. The doctor shook his head silently before disappearing.

"We did all we could to make this city a better place. We operated, we experimented, we did all we could to make you better, and what did we get as payment? Hounded out of here, beaten, and called freaks and sinners."

Russ' breathing slowed and he became cold, with cuts starting to appear on his skin and the blood dripping onto the dirty floor, but he didn't feel a single moment of pain.

"Do you see my scars? Beautiful, aren't they? I did them myself, and I wouldn't change them for the world, but those outside, those who didn't understand what we were doing here, came and ruined everything."

He couldn't move; all he could do was watch her as she spoke.

"They burned our work, beat us, and left us to die before locking up this place and never letting anyone open those doors again."

He felt his legs release, and he dropped to the floor, able to breathe normally again. When he looked up again, the doors were gone, but the entire basement was illuminated in a strange grey light, and the woman was in her uniform once more.

"And now, thanks to your coming here, I can begin my work once more. I may not have had the doctors here, but I watched them work. I may have stayed silent, but I learned their ways and their methods. Now I get to use them on you."

"Where's John?"

She laughed as if his question was the funniest thing she had heard.

"He's taken pride of place in my new collection, as will you when I am finished."

She waved a hand dismissively, and a beam of light moved across the floor and illuminated a large crucifix as it slowly simmered into being. Hanging from it, his hands and feet nailed to it, was John, his face covered in cuts and missing lumps of flesh.

The scream that burst forth from his mouth was animalistic in its anger and pain before he fell forward, landing on the dirty floor, unable to move.

Russ didn't know how much time passed, but she would appear and reappear in front of him, taunting and torturing him in equal measure, until, one day, she placed a loaded gun in his hand.

"One bullet. Survive, and you earn yourself a prize. Fail, and your skull will decorate my walls. I feel that's fair."

He had nothing left to lose, so he held the barrel of the gun against his temple. Russ pulled the trigger and felt strangely relieved that the only sound it made was the simple click of an empty barrel.

Laughing, the nurse disappeared, leaving Russ in a clumsy pile, covered in his own piss and tears. It was hopeless; there was no way he was going to get out of this place.

On the channel that he and John had created together, videos began to upload. Some of the empty rooms and some of the strange files that had been left open revealed the victims that had once sought treatment at the hospital.

It was one particular video that got attention. At first, the comments were insulting and called the scene fake or made up; some even said it was the worst special effects job that they had ever seen, but soon, it went viral.

That's when the authorities saw it and kicked down the doors to the hospital, going through each room they came to, but Russ was nowhere to be found, and neither was John. It was as if they had never existed, yet the videos continued, and the channel grew ever more successful.

The viewers became more rabid with each video posted, demanding more and more visceral forms of entertainment, and that is where the nurse's skills came in handy.

Each video, from there on in, was her putting Russ through some form of torture or experiment, but each one was written off as badly scripted, poorly filmed attempts at amateur horror shorts, but it served her well.

The building couldn't be knocked down; it was a historically listed building, and the videos brought more and more urban explorers, and that meant one thing.

Her experiments could continue forever.

Remember

Looking down at the uniform and the heaviness holding me where I stood, I couldn't help but wonder what was going on. So many decisions, so many moments, and not a single one was in my own control.

My own life didn't feel like it was controlled, or if it was, then it certainly wasn't by me. It didn't even seem to be in my hands, whether or not I was alive. It was all left to chance and the words of others.

Sometimes, just sometimes, a person will feel the moment that will turn out to be their last one on this earth. That's a scary thought in any moment, but, as I look around me, it's even worse when you're in the middle of a war zone.

Advancing, retreating, and holding the position were all the same. Death could and would come from anywhere at any time. From above, from below, from behind, and from the front.

Bullets, bombs, mines, and bayonets each brought with them a different level of pain and suffering. Some died quickly, others slowly and with screams stuck in the back of their throats. This was no way to live; it was certainly no way to die, that was for sure.

No matter how much I wished it to not be true, this was my moment, my last breath, my last minutes, maybe even my last few seconds, and I wasn't even sure that anyone would care.

As I stand here, talking to myself, another thought strikes me—one that cuts through me worse than anything the enemy could ever put me through. These are my last words, and I'm not even sure that you will ever hear them.

My feet were still rooted to the spot. If I squinted and squeezed my eyes shut tightly enough, I could make out the shapes of the enemy army. They looked like shadows, like walking and talking nightmares, with each of them bringing the promise of death. It wasn't a threat; it was a promise—a slow and creeping death—but why were they our enemy?

Was it because they were just from another country and we wanted something that they had?

Was it the colour of their skin or the tone of their accent?

Or was it just because of the orders of someone else, someone with more power and authority than I would ever wield in my entire life?

It didn't matter. Nothing would ever matter, not after the next few minutes passed. Why would I care? I wouldn't even be here, but one thing keeps nagging at the back of my mind. It was incessant; it was boring through my brain faster than a bullet from a rifle, and I couldn't stop thinking about it.

I saluted you without fail each and every time we crossed paths, sir. It was a matter of respect for me, a choice that I made, but would you have done the same for me? I doubt it. I'm not even sure you remembered my name, despite the multiple times I told you it, along with my rank and number.

That wasn't the only thing that seemed content, even eager, to get under my skin. It was the simple, undeniable fact that I followed each and every order you gave me with no flinching or hesitation. I followed them with my head high and my chest pushed out.

Back home—oh, yes, back home—was where my heart yearned to be, but it broke with each second that I wasn't able to be there. My friends, my family, even the people who lived on my street—I missed them all. I wondered if they ever thought of me or if I was merely something out of sight and out of mind to them. It was always so much quieter back then; we were lost in our own little worlds. We didn't know about countries invading and advancing to take what they wanted with force and violence. To put it simply, it wasn't our problem; it wasn't my problem. I was too wrapped up in running my little piece of land that I'd turned into a farm, and I wanted to be left alone to tend to my animals.

We all knew one another back there, and we all pulled together to get ourselves through any issue that stopped in front of us. It was simple, it was quiet, and it was safe. Much safer than where I am now.

Despite following all your orders and seeing all the things that no person should ever have to see, I am stuck here with no way to undo that. It was so unfair, so harsh, so endless.

I'm sinking into the mud, the excrement, the blood—all that has mixed to create some kind of hell that will eventually break us all. There was no way to survive it, no way to outrun it; it was inevitable the way it took hold of us all, its claws sinking into our flesh and bones.

I was outside yet felt like the world around me was closing in on me, threatening to squash me into some kind of paste, my organs and blood just adding to the mess that had hold of my scuffed and dented boots.

A wall of sound made it hard to concentrate on the words that were in my mind—words that I was speaking out loud despite there being nobody listening to me. The sounds of animal-like screams of pain, ones that, if I stayed alive for long enough, would haunt each nightmare I had left to dream.

Men were screaming out for their mothers, and to most, they were their last words ever spoken—not that it had made a difference. They were still in agony, their lives ebbing away while explosions threw mud in the air along with pieces of what I assume used to be friends of mine, people I had trained and come through the ranks with. I didn't want to think about their bodies being ripped apart, their limbs, their organs, decorating the mud, grass, and even dead bodies that were our surroundings.

Closing my eyes for a moment and wondering if this would be my last, I envisioned those lucky enough to be getting shipped home, although I wasn't sure lucky was the right word for them.

I could see it now. Bandages covering their ripped and torn faces, blood seeping through the fabric, and the pads designed to stem the flow. Some had limbs missing; others were carried on those horrible, uncomfortable stretchers that shook with each step the medics took. I wasn't even sure if they were alive or just the shells of the men they were before as they limped, their bodies leaning awkwardly on the stained, wooden crutches that they had been given.

The one thing that seemed out of place, even confusing, was the fact that all of this was somehow connected. It felt like I had the solution right in front of me, but it was just out of reach, and I hated it. I felt an anger twist, fester, and surge through each and every fibre of my being.

A voice screamed out in pain. Another man called out for his mother, for anyone who would listen to his anguish, but it was in vain. Nobody cared; they were too wrapped up in their own pain and suffering to worry about that of a nameless, and mostly faceless, soldier.

When it's my time, not that I get to choose, I won't call out. I don't see the need to do it. I don't even have anything left to call out.

But what about you?

I know it's a bit strange that I'm asking you that. It possibly doesn't even make a lick of sense, but, as a courtesy, hear me out.

What is going through your head right now?

Do you remember our names and faces, or are we just a glimpse, a shadow, of a memory in your brain?

To be honest, I'm not even sure I can remember the names and faces of all I've known throughout this pointless, vicious, endless war, but I can be forgiven for that. There was no point in me remembering any of them. They would be dead soon enough; they probably wouldn't even be in one piece, let alone alive and smiling next to me and holding up their rifle.

Do you feel any sorrow or guilt over the senseless slaughter that you sent us all into without warning?

I doubt that. We were nothing to you. No, that's not quite right. We were little tin soldiers for you to play with, like a little boy letting his imagination run away with him while moving their little toys back and forth.

Come on, sir. Let's be honest, and I mean really honest, with one another. You didn't give us a second thought, did you? When asked, you will say the losses were a regrettable but sad by-product of the war, but then go back to sitting behind your desk, safe and sound in the four walls that protected you from the bombs, the bullets, and the death that surrounded and followed the rest of us.

When you think of this time and this period in history, you won't remember us as you grow older. We won't remember you as we sacrifice our chances at growing older, all in the name of protecting our country. No, that's not what we were doing, was it? We're not protecting them; we were protecting you. We were protecting the assets that we hold and the status quo that keeps people like you in power.

You will shine your medals, each one given to you with a firm handshake and a smile, and feel like you did everything you could possibly do, but that isn't true, is it? You did as little as you had to.

In fact, you are just like me, aren't you? You just kept your head down and followed the orders of those above you. The one difference was that the orders didn't risk your life; they risked, and took, ours.

It was all connected; it always was.

Your safety. Your words. Your silence amongst the brutal violence of those around us.

But to you, that was okay. You would polish those medals and stare at them as they hung on your walls. You would put away those little tin men and those little tin soldiers you used to recreate the battles that you were most proud of.

Yes, you carry on doing that. It's what you always do, and it's what you always will do.

Now, on the other hand, I am in a country far from home. My feet are sinking even further into the mud where I stand, and I wait, now silent, for my heart to stop as I look down at the gaping wound in my chest, making quiet sucking noises.

Yes, this is my moment, my last words, and I was right. There was nobody to hear them.

Heart-Shaped

Describing the town of Long-View as secluded could be seen as being a little too polite. The word that should have been used was forgotten. It had been forgotten by all except those unlucky enough to live there.

On the surface, it looked like Long-View had nothing to offer in the way of entertainment either, but if you knew where to look, there was something for even the darkest of hearts.

Peculiar Pisces was a shop that catered to exactly that clientèle. It was a tiny shop that would be lucky to have enough space for more than two customers at a time, and even that was a tight squeeze.

The dusty shelves and tables creaked under the weight of their macabre contents. There were candles, statues, and anything even remotely strange, each with its own individual price tag.

Every relic had been carefully curated and held its own purpose. Some were obvious, others were only known to a certain few, but each waited patiently for their new owner to find them.

Jonathan had owned the shop since his early twenties and was intensely proud of everything he had collected and sold. Now, in his late forties, he had begun to grow despondent and bitter that there had been one thing that always seemed just out of reach.

The Heart-Shaped Box was something that had been spoken about in hushed tones amongst the various collectors he knew. It was something that somehow managed to both exist physically while sounding like a child's fairytale at the same time.

Some had said his obsession with the box and the other items in the shop had left Jonathan with somewhat of a reputation as a standoffish, morbid, and even eccentric person to be avoided at all costs. To some extent, that worked in his favour. It meant he could shut his shop whenever he wanted to, travel wherever he could to get new items, and then come back without having missed a single thing, but it was somewhat of a miserable and lonely existence.

Jonathan looked up, seeing the various candles giving the shop a rather dusty and dim look, and sighed. Another day without a single visitor or customer did, however, have a positive; it had given him time to read up more about the box and its history.

Each legend that mentioned the item, each fairytale, and each story were different. Some said that it was a cursed item, one that plagued its owners with nightmares so vivid that they would torment them to the point of insanity and self-harm.

Other stories told of it holding a special power, a magic of sorts, that would coat the owner and give them the ability to gain everything they wished for and to manipulate the people around them to that very end.

It didn't matter how many times Jonathan read the legends, he always managed to find some new little detail that made him even more determined to find it. He wasn't even sure if he believed the rumours of a curse or even the whisperings of it fulfilling the owner's every wish, but there was a compulsion, almost an obsession, to have it in his possession.

Placing the heavy book down on the desk in front of him, he realised that he'd placed his finger on a passage that he didn't remember having ever seen in the book before. His eyes were drawn to the words that seemingly beckoned him to come closer to the page.

For a moment, with each hesitation marked by the ticking of the ancient clock on the wall behind him, Jonathan just stared at the book and wondered if he was imagining it or if it was just the excitement making him want to read more. Taking a deep breath, he leaned forward and read the passage with his finger, tracing the space under each word.

Man eating orchids, razor-sharp baby's breath, and ever-tightening angel's hair. All things that have been purported to spring forth from the box itself. Could it be a figment of the imaginations of the nightmare-afflicted victims, or could it be the ramblings of the insane, used in an effort to prevent its discovery?

What a strange passage. It made no sense, and Jonathan, more than anything, was completely sure that he was writing it for the first time, which was impossible considering the age of the book. Closing it with a thud, he stood and waited for the aching pain in his back to stop before even attempting to move.

Each step felt heavier and more laboured than the last, but it didn't matter. The enjoyment of looking at his collection, running his fingers over each item, and feeling the energy each one held was like magic at his fingertips, dancing across his skin and through his body. It's one of the pleasures that came with being a person with a strong core of belief; it gave him the chance to be one with every bump and every imperfection that he felt.

As the night turned to pitch-black darkness, so had the weather. Rain lashed down against the windows of the shop, its rhythmic echoes bouncing around the shop as if vying for his attention. There wasn't anything particularly special about the weather this evening; Long-View had a reputation for not being somewhere to end up if you liked being dry and warm, but Jonathan couldn't help but feel transfixed by the patterns the rain made on the windows.

Opening the door, the bell jingled above him, and a rush of cold air pushed itself into the shop as he watched the storm.

In between the howling sounds of the wind and the forceful pitter-patter of the rain, Jonathan was sure that he could hear the faint sound of footsteps.

"Hello? Is anyone out there?"

When no reply came, he sighed and tried once more, regretting his decision to open the door.

"Do you need help? My shop isn't much to look at, but at least it's warm, dry, and sheltered."

For a split second, his voice seemed faint and hesitant to compete with the storm in an effort to be heard. Once more, his words went ignored, and he rolled his eyes.

"Fuck you then," he sighed before stepping back to close the door, only stopping when a small, dark parcel caught his attention. Despite its darkness, Jonathan was sure that he could see it glint at him, reminding him of a jewel. Reaching a hand out, a sudden sense of hesitation pushed itself through his thoughts, and he took a step back.

"Well, what do we have here?"

Jonathan had no reason to have asked the question out loud; after all, he was in the shop on his own, but he felt a strange comfort in having done so.

Glancing over his shoulder at the old clock on the wall, he listened to the ticking sound while trying to decide whether or not to bring the parcel inside. It wasn't the first time he had been left an unlabelled gift outside the store. Sometimes it was just the town youths playing a trick on him by wrapping up a dog turd or two, sometimes even a dead rat, but this was different.

"Just pick the damn thing up, you coward. It's a box. What's the worst thing it could be?"

Jonathan sighed at the quiet, awkward sound of his own voice.

"The first sign of madness is talking to yourself, and I guess I've nailed that one, at least."

Stepping forward with a nod, he grabbed the soaking wet parcel in his hands and knocked the shop door closed with his heel, the familiar sound of the bell above him acting like the soundtrack to his movements.

In his hands, the package felt heavy despite its small size. The dark cloth it had been wrapped in was soaked through, but, try as he might, Jonathan couldn't see through it as it dripped onto the wooden floor.

Rushing towards the table, ignoring the trail of rainwater he was leaving behind, Jonathan dropped the package with a thud. It just looked like any other wrapped-up box. The dark cloth had been tied in a neat and tidy bow; the whole thing looked rather professional, like the sort of parcel you'd get if you paid someone in a store to wrap a gift for you.

Running his fingers over the covering, Jonathan was surprised to find that it didn't feel like any cloth he'd ever touched before. It was somehow smooth, yet it tried to cling to his finger as he tried to untie the bow. The cloth fell away, revealing a small, well-polished box with a metal clasp on it, but that wasn't what had drawn his attention.

The box was a perfectly carved heart shape, and on top, in an inlay, was a small photograph of a young woman looking back at him. She had the most piercing pair of hazel eyes that Jonathan had ever seen and a beautifully disarming smile. Instantly, it felt like he had known the unnamed woman all his life. A sense of familiarity prickled at the back of his mind, but somehow he knew he had never met her before.

Jonathan rubbed his eyes and looked at her again. Once more, he was captivated by the beauty of the box and the photograph, allowing an unexplainable sense of connection to run through him. The more he looked at it, the more aware he became of a quiet crackling noise emanating from the wood.

Curiosity gnawed at his mind, compelling him to delve deeper into the origins of the box and the photo that had been inserted into the lid. Guided by an impulse that he was powerless to resist, he ran his fingers over the wood but jumped back slightly when one of the panels clicked loudly and opened.

When he was sure that it wasn't going to move any more, Jonathan noticed that an address was carved deeply into the wood and recognised it instantly. It was the address of a dilapidated old mansion on the outskirts of town. So far, it was less magical and more cliché, but the obsession he felt about the box silenced the voice at the back of his mind telling him to throw it away.

"Looks like I'm taking a trip then," he said to the photograph in the box as he picked it up, holding it against his chest. The slight vibrations coming from the wood mixed with the excited beating of his heart.

***

Pulling up to the mansion, Jonathan felt a surge of pity for the old place. It had clearly been something to behold in its glory days. A building that no doubt held stories of a hundred lives or more. A building that people would have spoken about excitedly, feeling honoured to have gained an invite.

There was an eerie silence that surrounded the building, despite the storm raging. Watching as the lightning cast twisted, misshaped shadows, he couldn't help but wonder why he'd come to this place. It made no sense that the box had been sent from here. Nobody had lived in the mansion for as long as he could remember. It was just a broken, bent shell of itself.

Getting out of the car, Jonathan shuddered at the heavy atmosphere in the air around him. He could feel a strange, just out of sight, presence that made the hairs on the back of his neck stand on end.

The closer he came to the mansion, if it really could still be called that, the more hesitant he became. It didn't matter that the rain lashing against him was soaking him to the bone; it didn't matter that he felt colder than he had ever felt before; he just stood in front of the once grand entrance and tried to force himself to take one more step.

Pressing a hand against the door, it slowly opened with the deafening creak of rusty hinges, and he stared straight ahead. The hallway in front of him was strangely illuminated, but he couldn't make out where the light was coming from.

"Hello? Can anyone hear me?"

The sound of his own voice was soon lost in the looming space in front of him, punctuated by a loud crack of thunder. In the blink of an eye, he was standing in the hallway, and the door shut loudly behind him.

"What the...?"

Jonathan was sure that he hadn't taken a single step since standing in front of the building, but here he was, looking around him at the mould-covered walls, faded paintings, and cracks that seemed to criss-cross every available surface.

After trying the door and finding it locked, he knew that there was only one thing left to do. Stop his imagination from running wild. The mansion was old; the door frame had probably just warped, and that was why the door wouldn't budge. That's all it was. There wasn't some benevolent force keeping him here. He'd read too many legends and myths, and again, his mind was playing tricks on him like it always did.

Closing his eyes shut for a moment and taking his time to count to ten, Jonathan could feel his heartbeat growing frantic in his chest and knew, in that moment, that coming here had been a mistake. It was too late now. He was here; he had the box, and now he needed to find out how the two were connected. This could be the answer to all the questions he'd had over the years. This could be the happy ending to his obsessive search for the box. He just had to be sensible about all of this.

He opened his eyes and took a clumsy step forward, cringing at the loudness of the floorboards creaking beneath his feet. He'd seen enough horror movies over the years to know what to expect from a place like this, especially if this was someone from town pranking him again, but deep down, there was something eerie about the whole thing, and he felt compelled to get to the bottom of it all. He had to know why he was here, why the box was left on his doorstep in the pouring rain, and who the person in the photograph was.

Each room he came to seemed like a copy of the one that came before it, but with one severe difference: the level of dankness and decay. With each room, he began to feel dirtier and colder, like he was invading some dark moment in time that he should never have seen.

It was the paintings that spooked him the most. Their eyes were lifeless, soulless even, and followed him around each room he went into. It felt like they were judging each step he took and each decision he made.

Swiftly moving from room to room, fighting the urge to pocket some of the strange statues and trinkets that he saw had been left behind, Jonathan started to hear the faint sound of whispering. At first, the voices were almost unintelligible, and he shivered. This had to be some kind of pre-Halloween joke, surely, but even if it was, it just wasn't funny. At all.

Jonathan looked up and saw that he had come to a twisted staircase in the middle of a large space. Looking around, he could see that every inch of the walls were covered with yet more paintings, each one matching the ones he had seen in the other rooms, but these were as clean as if they had only just been painted.

Testing the first step with the tip of his shoe to see if it would hold his weight, he couldn't help but feel a slight tinge of excitement running through his body as his obsessive need to explore and discover rushed through his mind. If this was where the box really came from, then it would be priceless. The other collectors, the other people in the groups he frequented, would look upon him with jealousy at such a unique discovery. He would be a hero among them.

Before he knew it, he had scared the twisting, turning staircase, ignoring the noise of the metal and wood straining under the weight of its first user in what must have been decades at least.

With a new-found sense of confidence, he threw the large, heavy double doors in front of him open and gasped.

The room was vast and stretched as far as his eyes could see. It looked impossibly large, like a disjointed, warped painting.

Each one of the walls was adorned with decaying, rotten roses, each with a thorny stem that seemed to sway in rhythm with the pounding of his heartbeat. In the centre of the room, seemingly taking pride of place amongst its surroundings, stood a dusty, cobweb-covered Victrola playing a hauntingly familiar melody, the voices drifting around Jonathan and out into the hallway. Next to it was a small, but ornate, table.

Making his way closer, Jonathan noticed that there was a box atop the table that matched the one he had received on his doorstep, save for one difference. This one was pitch black as if it had been burned, but its surface was smooth like a jewel.

Without warning, the box he had been holding in his hands turned to ash instantly, its grains drifting through his fingers and falling to the carpeted floor, leaving only the photograph, untouched, in the palms of his hands.

Compelled by an indescribable force, while holding onto the photo with the other hand, he reached out and opened the tarnished, heart-shaped box on the table, revealing its contents. An old, faded photograph that, except for its aged condition, mirrored the one he'd received earlier.

Instantly, the room filled with a chill presence, as if the demons from his worst nightmares had started to take shape in front of his very eyes. Each creature, each dark, shadow-like thing, shifted, moved, and formed into angle after angle, shape after shape, until it became a perfectly translucent vision of the woman in the photograph.

Silence took over the room as the music stopped as soon as she tilted her head to look at him. Jonathan couldn't take his eyes away from her; she was as truly beautiful as she had been in the photographs, but there was something in the way her eyes bore through him that made him want to turn and run.

"You came to open the box, so tell me, what is it your heart desires?"

The voice. It was the same one that had been singing the song from the Victrola, but it was different; the question was more of a threat than a real effort to know what he wanted.

Consumed by fear, Jonathan turned on his heel and tried to run, but the spectral woman's grip tightened around him, her icy fingers digging into his flesh. The more he struggled, the louder the voices in his mind became. Nightmarish visions ran in front of his eyes of his family suffering in front of him, but he was powerless to help them. It showed all his misdeeds and all the people he had hurt throughout his life, all jeering violently at him.

His mind began to fill with their screams and jeers, as well as the anguished cries for help from the other souls held within the box.

Flesh began to peel from his body, leaving a burning, searing pain to force a scream from his lips as his skin was flayed from him in a cloud of blood and muscle.

Feeling himself lifted into the air, the weightless sensation carried Jonathan to the box, and he hovered above it, blood dripping from his carcass.

"You men are all the same. Show you a pretty face, offer the faintest whisper of power, and you drop all resemblance of intelligence as you trip over yourself to snatch it all for yourself."

Jonathan's body cracked and twisted into obscene angles before being pulled into the depths of the box, with the woman allowing one last scream of pain to escape his lips, much to her amusement.

Safe in the knowledge that she had taken another soul for herself, the spectre dissipated, but she could still sense everything in the mansion. Every sound, every movement, and every item held within its walls were hers.

Days turned to weeks, and the weeks turned to months, and barring a brief and lazy search by the tiny police force from town, Jonathan was lost in an eternal nightmare, fated to stay in the clutches of the cursed relic. His once rational mind, one full of facts and knowledge, was now fractured and broken, with only agonising pain to keep it company.

And so, the heart-shaped box continued to haunt the mansion and its grounds, with its whispers carried on the wind, luring unsuspecting strangers into her clutches. Some she used to place the false boxes with their clues at the doorsteps of those desperate enough to want to believe it could give them everything their selfish hearts desired; others she just toyed with until their minds broke and she left them discarded like cheap broken toys.

Jonathan was soon forgotten and, as the years passed, became a cautionary tale that then morphed into little more than an urban legend told around camp-fires and during Halloween sleepovers. Just another victim of the heart-shaped box.

That was the magic that inherently lived throughout time. It kept the world turning and lives being lived. Things were soon forgotten, and if they weren't, well, they were soon melded into something unbelievable—a bedtime story here, a bedtime story there. That kind of thing.

It had happened throughout the entire existence of the human race. History became legends, legends became myths, myths became morality plays, and so on. It would never change, for it had no need to.

The Heart-Shaped Box, that was something that lived the same existence. The woman's name had long been lost to the sands of time, but all she knew was that she needed fresh souls to stop her from fading away like those who had come before her.

It was a good lesson, really, something to teach those who would listen. A person was never fully forgotten until every effect that their existence had on the world had faded away, and just like that, she'd found a way to cheat the system.

The more souls she took, the more of an effect she had on the world. Each ripple that came from her actions kept her alive, to a certain extent, and the fact that it came at the cost of a stupid, selfish man's obsession with power? All the better for it. Besides, it's not like they would be missed.

Printed in Great Britain
by Amazon

30125398R00099